Protecting those you love in an x-rated world

Protecting those you love in an x-rated world

Blocking Harmful Media and Online Influences

by
Michele Washam
and **Tom Mooty**

Bridge-Logos
Orlando, Florida 32822

Bridge-Logos

Orlando, FL 32822 USA

Protecting Those You Love in an X-rated World
by Michele Washam and Tom Mooty

Printed in the United States of America.

Library of Congress Catalog Card Number: 2007929821
International Standard Book Number 978-0-88270-443-2

G1.316.N.m706.35250

Contents

10 Things This Book Will Help You Understand

1. This book contains dozens of proven ways to safeguard your home, your family, and your computer against pornography.

2. The author, a former producer of Internet pornography, socialized with hackers, conversed with actors while they were working, and negotiated with the flesh brokers out West for content. She knows what she's talking about.

3. The author, now a Christian for many years, has become an informed and dangerous freedom fighter for the body of Christ. *Learn how you can become one as well.*

4. You don't have all the answers you might think you have! You need solid help and understanding. This book contains the steps to help anyone.

5. How to break the ice every week, even daily, to talk to your kids about sex-related things.

6.Perhaps you're wondering what you did to contribute to the situation you may be facing with your spouse. The author says, "Probably not much, if anything at all." Rather than dwell on guilt/blame, just focus on doing the best things you can to help.

7. Where to find help. This book contains a comprehensive list of where to turn for help and support for pornography addictions and help for families who have been affected by addiction.

8. How to know if someone in your house is visiting inappropriate websites.

9. Ten ways to arm yourself with the proper equipment to block out pornography.

10. Four important things you can do to prepare yourself to pray and receive God's peace in the battle you are facing.

Introduction

I have worked with Michele Washam as her editor on this important book. She has presented a wealth of information and knowledge here that can help you recognize when pornography has invaded your home, how to talk to your kids about it, how to protect your home as a single parent, and how to pray and fight for the freedom of an addicted spouse.

It wasn't always easy for me to work with this material, but I believe that this is an important book that can help anyone whose life has been touched by the pain and evil of pornography. This author speaks as an insider, one who has worked in designing pornographic websites and the promotion of pornography. She knows what she's talking about.

Since becoming a Christian several years ago, however, Michele has devoted herself to helping people break this addiction. Inside these pages, she offers invaluable insight and information to help parents and spouses learn what they can do on their own and, most important of all, how to cooperate *with* God in freedom fighting for their loved ones.

Michele has listed the various avenues of pornography, explaining that each form of pornographic media is fine tuned to provide a special fantasy for anyone even slightly tempted or curious to delve deeper. Once they've hooked their prey, it's a true battle to set them free. Sadly, pornography from several of these sources has infected the body of Christ.

Pornography addiction begins in the wounded and needy human soul (mind, will, and emotions) that seeks sources of stimulation and temporary relief from a broken life's pressures. Once the needy soul drags someone into the underworld of pornography, the body becomes involved in the addiction. Such a powerful mind-body agreement can be very difficult to break, but it can be done! This is a book you need to read, even if you do not think any area of your life has been touched by this insidious evil. Knowledge of evil is one thing—knowing how to best fight the evil turns that knowledge into wisdom.

—Rev. Liberty Savard (Author of fourteen books published by Bridge-Logos Publishers on overcoming the power of the unsurrendered soul with the Keys of the Kingdom.)

1

From Peddling Porn to Ministering to Broken Hearts

From Porn To Faith

I was born in 1968 in Buffalo, New York, to a large and loving Italian Catholic family. My mom, Rose, was a housewife and my dad, Bill, owned a remodeling business which we all helped out in at one time or another. By the time I was nine years old I knew how to answer my dad's business phones and dispatch his crews on the two-way radios as efficiently as any of his other employees.

In 1968 the television shows were relatively innocent, moral, and entertaining: the *Here's Lucy* show, *Hawaii Five-O*, *The Mod Squad*, and *60 Minutes* made their debut that year. The soap opera, *One Life To Live*, made its entrance that year as well—it's amazing how far today's soap operas have moved from those days, isn't it? *Lost In Space*, the *Lucy* show, and the *Andy Griffith* show all made an exit that same year and went on to become television legends in the eyes of some, and many of us "old people" still watch the re-runs. Television was different back then.

The Vietnam War was the hot topic, Richard Nixon was nominated to run for president by the Republican National Convention in Miami Beach and later that year went on to win the presidency. We put a man on the moon in 1968 and listened to hollow-sounding audio broadcasts as they spoke to us from a world away. Sadly, Martin Luther King was assassinated the same year and many people still wonder if 1968 wasn't the beginning of the end of an America built on tradition, morals, and family values. Forty years have passed and the massive changes in society, technology, morals, and attitudes are all reasons why I have felt the need to write this book.

How well do I remember coming home from school where my mom always had a snack waiting and a wonderful smell would greet me at the door of whatever delicious dinner she was whipping up for her family. The families who surrounded us made our neighborhood one of the warmest places in the world to many of us who grew up there. Back then, tradition still defined life growing up in the Italian, Irish, Jewish, and Polish families that made that west-side neighborhood a landmark in my childhood memories.

Although many of my childhood friends came from different ethnic backgrounds, the "old country" values we were all taught were the same. We had respect for our elders, we ate dinner together as a family every night (even if it meant packing it up and bringing it to Dad's office on the rare evening he had to work late), and our parents looked out for other peoples' kids as if they were their own. Moms protected everybody's kids from dangers such as crossing the street alone, staying out past the switching on of the street lights, and being outside without shoes on (you never knew when you could step on broken glass!).

One of the most serious infractions of those days was going into a friend's house without telling your mother in case she called your name and you didn't hear her (there were no cell phones back then, just Mother's loud call). This sense of family unity is surely what earned Buffalo its reputation of being the "City of Good Neighbors."

Some people say that Buffalo has two seasons, winter and almost winter. That's not true. Although the winters are brutally cold and bring more snow than most folks could fathom; spring, summer, and fall all have special characteristics that make Buffalo a place to keep going back "home" to if only for short visits. Those visits invariably include revisiting gourmet delights like Anchor Bar chicken wings, LaNova Pizza, and Sahlen's famous hot dogs. In the summertime, when Lake Erie finally melted and the warm air blanketed the city, our family would load up a car or two with baskets of snacks, grandparents, aunts, uncles, and cousins to head over the Peace Bridge into Canada for a day at Niagara Falls. Just imagine, we traveled to a "foreign" country for a day trip and visited one of the wonders of the world for the cost of a twenty-five cent toll and a tank of gas.

In the autumn when the leaves started to change, we'd load cars with the same family members and baskets of snacks and head out to the country. The "country" was anything outside the city where you could see nothing but trees and fields. Most often we'd end up in the Allegheny Mountains where we'd stop along the way and pick apples and Garduni (burdock to some)—a wild plant that's used to make an Italian side dish I can't even begin to explain.

During the holidays, our entire family gathered at my grandmother's house where she spent hours over the stove cooking lasagna, turkey, homemade ravioli, and cannolis. As each of my girl cousins and I reached the age where we could help cook, we stood shoulder to shoulder with her, learning the recipes passed on to her from past generations. To this day, I still cook the Sunday afternoon sauce like my mom and grandmother did using the two-hundred-year-old recipe that made its way through several generations beginning back in northern Italy.

The aroma still brings back memories of days gone by and my family still gathers on Sunday afternoons to enjoy each other over the meal. As with most Italian families, all major events—whether good or bad, happy or sad—revolve around the kitchen table.

Florida—Promise of a Tropical Paradise

In 1981 my uncle came back from a trip to Florida and mesmerized my parents with stories of a tropical paradise where it never snowed and prosperity was found in abundance. It wasn't long after that visit that my parents decided to sell our home and move to south Florida. I was twelve years old when my mom loaded us into the car and we drove out of Buffalo. It took me over a year to adjust to the move and on more than one occasion, I packed my little suitcase and threatened to run away and go back "home." Although I've grown up since and now live in Tennessee, Buffalo will always be the "home" of my heart.

In 1990, while living in south Florida, I met my first husband and married him a year later. It's funny how we can look back in life and recognize times when God was trying to guide us but we were too busy doing our own thing to listen to that still, small voice of His. I knew when I was walking down the church aisle at my great big Italian wedding that I shouldn't be marrying him. The funny thing is, as my dad was holding my arm and leading me to the altar, he said "Are you sure you want to do this?"

"Dad ... it's a little late for that," I whispered from under my veil.

"No, it isn't," he replied, "If you want to change your mind, we're out of here." My dad knew I was making a mistake.

I probably would have turned and ran if I hadn't felt guilty for all the money and time my parents had invested in the wedding, not to mention the 200 people who were sitting there with eyes riveted on me. So I kept walking down the aisle, and five years and three kids later, I went against every "rule" in my family's book and filed for divorce. About the same time, in 1995, my grandfather was diagnosed with terminal cancer back home. There was really no question about what we needed to do. My father sold his telephone business where I had spent the previous ten years working for him, and our family went back home to Buffalo.

Going back to Buffalo in January after living in Florida for almost fifteen years was a shock to my system. The bitter cold and four feet of snow on the ground were a reminder of why I had never moved back permanently. But my Papa was sick and needed us, so I looked beyond the cold and focused on family.

In 1995, the Internet began to evolve and involve people all around the world. I was married with three children and a myriad of responsibilities, but I became totally enamored with this new electronic window to the world, the "Information Superhighway" as it was first called. I became so addicted to the Internet that I soaked up every single thing I could learn about how to use a computer, design a Web page, market products online, and anything else that related to that. I was hooked.

Highway to Trouble

Addiction is a pretty powerful word to use in this situation, but I was genuinely addicted to the Internet's possibilities. My refusal to recognize this and my adamant refusal to allow anything to limit or interfere with my time online, plus the fact that I already believed I had married the wrong man anyway, pushed my marriage into its final stages. With my divorce in the works, I moved on and he moved back to Florida.

He was gone, the computer was always turned on, and I felt I had the world at my fingertips.

I took off out of that gate like a race horse only to run directly into the arms of my next big mistake—mistake number two: short, stocky, and cunningly smart "Shaun." I truly believed that this man was absolutely *the* one for me. So I set off to Delaware where he lived to be with him. Once I was settled in Delaware, I started my own business designing Web pages. Before long I was making good money at doing something I really liked. Could things get any better?

Then a friend began telling me about all of the money that could be made by owning and operating a porn site. I listened to this friend—big mistake number three! That was one of those turning points that you hear about in people's lives; it was a really bad turning point in mine! You would think that with my upbringing and old-fashioned values that I would have known better. I *did* know better. To this day I still search for some hidden reason or trigger that caused me to make this choice, and sadly, as dumb as it sounds, I did it for the money.

There was no trauma in my past, no lack of material things (my dad was a good provider), I wasn't abused or neglected. And I had no fascination with pornography or erotic material. I just made a really bad choice thinking it was a good financial move. My thoughts at the time were focused on taking care of three kids without relying on the welfare system or a man. So, as dumb as it sounds, I temporarily sold out on my cherished values for the almighty dollar. Lots of them. Dear God, what was I thinking?

Although I was raised Catholic, I hadn't been to Mass in years, and confession was out of the question at that point in my life, but I still had a slight tinge of conscience. I knew it was wrong to even consider what I was thinking about doing, but the money was very tempting to a single mom. It was beyond tempting, it was flat-out calling to me. It was easy for me to rationalize why it would be okay. Being so far away from my parents and their influence made the decision to step into the seedy side of the Net easier than if I had been back home where they could have caught on to my activities.

I gave in to the temptation, totally ignoring the gut feeling I felt. I proceeded to build one of the world's first, ladies-only, erotic websites called just4ladies.com. It was an immediate success and women from all over the world began buying memberships for $39.99 per month. My site also had a large homosexual male clientele. The money rolled in whether I was awake or asleep, and life was looking pretty darn good from my pocket book's perspective.

It wasn't long before I decided to start designing regular adult websites for clients. Soon there were over a dozen of my sites online all raking in a good number of male clients who were all spending their $39.99 each month. I earned an average of $24,000 for each site built plus a portion of the membership fees. I was thinking, "Could life get any better than it is now?"

Live-In Fiancé—Mr. Mistake Number Two

My live-in fiancé at the time, Mr. Mistake Number Two, was only too happy to spend the money I was making. He enjoyed visiting my websites and even started suggesting ideas for content. He would spend hours online talking to the women in the live chat rooms. After dinner he would go into the chat rooms, and I would go to work designing and maintaining more sites and more chat rooms. He chatted, I worked, and the money rolled in like clockwork. The only other thing I had to do was to keep hiding it all from my children and my family.

My extremely traditional Italian Catholic parents would never have understood nor approved of what I was doing. I knew that I would be disowned by them if they found out. But that didn't stop me.

I was still marketing to women, but now I also marketed pornography to men: single men, married men, and engaged men. I marketed porn to men with kids and men without kids. The sites were being visited by businessmen who loved to spend their money on live girls and expensive videos. The married men usually just settled for the erotic pleasures that a regular membership provided. It didn't matter to me, not as long as they had a credit card. I never once looked beyond the Master Card to see that somewhere in the background there was probably a woman who was suffering greatly because of my desire to make money.

Somehow I was in denial of the fact that I was contributing to the decay of untold numbers of families. It is heartbreaking to me now that I never considered that I was causing so many hearts to break while bragging about how "good-looking" my websites were.

The Game Was Over

Right up until the time I was asked to write this book, I didn't really understand how the experience of my past could help other people. After becoming a Christian in June of 1999, my ministry revolved around fixing heartbreaks. But little by little my mind opened up to the situations and choices that led me to writing this book and to you, and I really began understanding that pornography is always a creator of heartbreak.

Before this, it took a life-changing heartbreak to finally get my attention. When this situation ripped through my life, it was the most painful thing I had ever dealt with. Shaun (not his real name) and I had been living together for almost three years when I began to feel that it was definitely time to make things official. I thought that I loved him more than the air I was breathing and I treated him like a king. I have no idea why I kept treating him that way when he showed me so little respect. I didn't seem to care, because I felt I would rather have him with his faults than be without him. After much nagging and threatening, he finally gave me a ring that he purchased with my money.

I deceived myself into believing that it didn't matter who paid for my ring. We were an official couple! What was his was mine and what was mine was his. I was pretty blind at the time because what was actually his and mine were all his, period.

Ring firmly planted on my finger, I got him to agree to relocate from Delaware to South Florida where I could be closer to my family. That June still stands out in my mind as we made plans to go down to Florida for two weeks to look for a home. Although Shaun couldn't leave until Friday, the kids and I left on Wednesday. I was so excited! I was making more money than I could ever spend, I was engaged to the most incredible man, and I was moving close to my family.

I hadn't even thought about what I would tell my family that I was doing for a living. But on the surface, I had everything I could possible want. How ignorant I was back then.

I have heard people talk about having a sixth sense, and I have heard some even say they had a "premonition" of things to come. I didn't believe in those things, and I certainly wouldn't have been looking for any warning signs from Heaven. Heaven was the farthest thing from my mind back then. Nonetheless, God was showing Himself to me even if I was ignoring Him.

The first warning sign God gave me at that time came in the form of a dream. If I wasn't a fanatic about journaling, I would have missed it altogether. One afternoon out of the blue I felt myself getting extremely tired. This was highly unusual because most days I easily worked for sixteen hours or more. I thought I might be getting sick and went to lie down for a while. I soon fell asleep, and as I slept, I had a vivid dream of Shaun, myself, and my children in a home watching an enormous tornado heading straight for us. The tornado hit us head on in the dream, and then I woke up.

To this day I can still remember every detail of that dream. It wasn't until much later that I learned from a preacher that God sometimes gives us warnings in our dreams. The preacher also told me that a tornado in a dream could symbolize life-changing, catastrophic events in the near future. At the time, I didn't take it as a warning sign; I just kept going.

The second warning sign I had from God came from my journal writings. Two days before I was due to leave for Florida, I wrote in my journal that I was packed and ready to go. I had reserved a limo for the trip to the airport and I had left Shaun with enough precooked meals to eat until he left that Friday. At the end of my entry—the last one

I would make—I wrote: "Everything is packed and we're ready to go. Shaun will be coming on Friday ... I hope."

I hope? What was that all about? Everything was good between us, wasn't it? Somewhere in the back of my mind, though, I knew it was the end; I just didn't listen. I kept on going.

The kids and I flew to Florida where my parents were happy to receive us. While waiting for Shaun to come, I went boating with my kid brother, hung out at the pool, and just enjoyed the Florida sunshine. The night before Shaun was due to arrive, I called to find out what time his flight would get in so I could pick him up. Strangely, he wasn't home. By ten o'clock that evening, I was panicking. I thought something had happened to him. One of his friends e-mailed me and told me he probably just went out with the guys and not to worry. I tried my best not to.

At 11:19 P.M. on June 19, 1999, my whole life came crashing down. The phone at my parents' house rang and the caller I.D. showed that it was Shaun. My heart sank as I sensed something was going to happen that I wasn't going to feel good about. "Hello," I answered.

"Michele? It's me. I just wanted to call and tell you that I'm not coming tomorrow. I don't love you anymore. You'll need to come and get all your stuff out of the townhouse because I am giving it up." Then, silence.

I felt my heart break inside of me. I also felt like a knife had just been plunged deep into my chest. I asked him what he meant in an attempt to stall him so I could collect myself. I thought a few seconds would give me time to recover from the blow he had just dealt me. "Shaun, what are you talking about? You loved me when I left Wednesday! How can that change in two days?"

"I don't love you anymore, and I don't want to raise any kids. I have to go now; just get your stuff out of the townhouse." Click ... and the line went dead. I never heard from him again. My life went crashing to the floor at 11:19 P.M. on June 19, 1999. Isn't it amazing how we can remember the precise time of certain events in our lives? I even remember seeing the tears on my shirt and thinking to myself, "My tears are staining my shirt." It was a moment I will never forget.

I didn't sleep a wink that night. The next morning my dad loaded me onto a plane, and we headed back to Delaware to collect the material pieces of my life. I remember very little of my trip back to Delaware. Just one memory stands out about that flight and that was that I felt like I was in a nightmare. I just wanted to close my eyes and sleep; it hurt too much to stay awake.

I remember the concern on my dad's face. He was determined to be strong and carry me through the worst event of my life, but deep down inside I knew he was angry with Shaun for what he had done. During the flight I remember laying my head against the wall of the plane; in my mind's eye, I was leaning against an angel. I can remember waves of pain washing over me, but that angel stayed right there. I didn't know it, but God was already catching me as I fell.

And I was falling hard.

2

Calling on the Power of Calvary— Help from Heaven

End or Beginning? God Knew

I was about to begin a long journey to recovery, but I didn't know it. The day I met the Lord was supposed to be the last day of my life. At 7:00 P.M. on June 27, 1999, I told my parents I was going to walk on the beach. I looked at them for what I thought would be the last time, silently asking them to forgive me for the pain I was about to cause them. I walked out their front door believing I would never come back, and headed toward the beach a couple of blocks away.

As I was walking down the Palm Beach inlet, I decided that I was just going to keep on going. I was going to walk right off the end of the inlet, and I didn't care what drowning might end up feeling like. I was sure that nothing could hurt more than my heart did at that moment.

Right before the inlet drops into the Atlantic Ocean it comes alongside a sandy beach known as Singer Island. For whatever reason, I turned left there and started walking down the beach. It was dusk and the beach was empty. I was alone. I'm not completely sure what made me turn off onto the sand, but I figured my plan could wait just a few minutes longer.

As I walked along the beach that evening, my heart overflowed with sorrow. Then I stopped walking and sat down on the sand. I turned and looked out over the ocean. It was beautiful, all pink and purple and blue from the reflection of the sunset. As I looked out at such beauty, I started crying my heart out to God.

"God! If You are really there and You can hear me, please help me. Oh, God, please help me!" The tears flowed from my eyes and my heart as I sat there reaching out for a God I hadn't acknowledged in a long, long time. I begged Him to fix this situation. I prayed He would bring Shaun back. I cried out to Him to stop my pain. My whole body was shaking from crying so hard.

After what felt like forever, but was really only a few minutes, I slowly stopped crying and a strange calm crept over me. Then the tears stopped and everything went still. It was at that very moment that I met the Lord. Filled with a peace I didn't have just seconds before, I heard God whisper His promise into my heart, *"Learn what I have to teach you and I will give you the miracle your heart seeks."* That was the moment that He planted the mustard seed of faith into my heart, and my life would never be the same again.

Some people might say that God doesn't talk to us like that anymore. Some people might believe that He never did. But when you have truly come to a point in your life where the only solution is our Heavenly Father and you are finally ready to hear Him, you will. His isn't a booming voice from the sky; it is a soft whisper in your heart and you'll never forget the first time you hear it. I wish I could convince everyone to just tilt their ear and open their hearts to His gentle, loving whisper; the world would never be the same.

That evening I walked back to my parents' house and for the first time since Shaun's devastating call, I had hope. Then, right before my eyes, a huge bright rainbow appeared in the sky. God had just affirmed His promise to me and I knew it. From that day forward, rainbows have held a special meaning for me. To this day, the Lord has never failed to come through for me and show me a rainbow!

Journey to Recovery

The first thing necessary for a journey to recovery is faith. If faith is new to you, a little guidance can go a long way. God is good; He always sends us a helper or two to fill the gap as we start our journey. Unbeknown to me, my first helper on my journey was the angel God promised He would send to watch over me. I didn't know that until a few months later and when I realized it, my heart burst with joy at the revelation. My second helper was the Catholic patron saint Jude Thaddeus, the intercessor for hopeless cases. I was hopeless all right!

The first Helper you have is our Heavenly Father who wants nothing more than to see you defeat whatever evil might be trying to destroy you and your family. Through this book, God has also sent another helper to try to answer some of the questions you may have while inspiring you with His promises and what they hold for you. I want you to meet Pastor Tom Mooty who will sprinkle his words of wisdom along the way and give you insight I think you'll be happy to receive. He's a man after God's own heart and he'll be helping us on this journey to restore and repair your heart. I want to let Pastor Tom speak for himself.

Note from Pastor Tom: Being in the ministry for thirty-eight years has yielded a lot of great experiences—and some that were not so great, but all of them have been interesting. I had always thought that I would write a book one day. Baptist pastors always have a lot of good stories.

Then my friend Michele Washam came to me with an idea and a passion so compelling that I agreed to join her in writing this book. When I discussed it first with my family, one of my three children asked me, "Dad, what do you know about pornography?" This was a logical question for a pastor's daughter to ask.

So, what do I know about pornography? I know that the genesis of the word *pornography* comes from the Greek word *pornay* which is a noun form of *pernao* meaning to sell. Another noun form *porneia* is defined as fornication, whoredom, concubinage, adultery, lewdness, or uncleanness. Still another verb form, *porneuo*, means to commit fornication or whoredom or practice adultery. (*The Analytical Greek Lexicon*; Zondervan; Grand Rapids, Michigan).

There is definitely an ancient and biblical tie between pornography and all forms of lewd behavior. No wonder the biblical writers warned everyone to stay away from this stuff! For example, we are told several times in Scripture to cleanse ourselves of the residue and filth of the flesh:

Galatians 5:16, *"This I say then, Walk in the Spirit, and ye shall not fulfil the lust of the flesh"* (KJV).

Second Corinthians 7:1, *"Having therefore these promises, dearly beloved, let us cleanse ourselves from all filthiness of the flesh and spirit, perfecting holiness in the fear of God"* (KJV).

Our flesh in itself is not evil and was in fact given to us by God Himself. But we are not to become slaves to the works of our flesh. We are told in Scripture that we are to crucify (kill) the desires of the flesh which can so easily dominate us. For example:

Exodus 20:14, *"Thou shalt not commit adultery"* (KJV).

Matthew 5:28, *"But I say unto you, That whosoever looketh on a woman to lust after her hath committed adultery with her already in his heart"* (KJV).

While adultery is usually described as a sexual uncleanness between married persons, it is also "looking on a woman to lust after her." This Scripture applies to lusting after women in books, magazines, movies, in person at the beach or on the street even though these scenarios did not exist in the times of the writing of Scripture. Do not forget the Biblical pronouncement of what happens when we yield to "the desires of the flesh."

James 1:14-15, *"But every man is tempted, when he is drawn away of his own lust, and enticed. Then when lust hath conceived, it bringeth forth sin: and sin, when it is finished, bringeth forth death"* (KJV).

Fornication (*porneia*) includes all forms of sexual impurity whether pre-marital, post-marital, mental, emotional—all forms of sexual immorality.

First Corinthians 6:18 tells us: *"Flee fornication. Every sin that a man does is without the body; but he that committeth fornication sinneth against his own body"* (KJV).

Ephesians 5:3, *"But fornication, and all uncleanness, or covetousness, let it not be once named among you, as becometh saints"* (KJV).

Sex is a part of life, given by God to be used within marriage to procreate the human race and for marital pleasure. There is nothing wrong with sex as long as it is used within the marriage relationship:

"Marriage is honourable in all, and the bed undefiled: but whoremongers and adulterers God will judge" (Hebrews 13:4, KJV).

I've counseled couples through real-life experiences with marriages in trouble. I am aware of the vast amounts of money spent on looking at pornography, money that has been taken from families. Have I seen pornography? Yes, I have seen some aspects of the industry, enough to know that it is bad news. The occasional miscue in typing in a website name has yielded pop-up after pop-up. In some cases, you wonder if will ever get out of the loop of all those ads and websites.

I am aware that pornography is called a "victimless crime." Wrong! Being under the influence of pornography has, in fact, led to the commission of many crimes with more and more occurring every day.

Dr. James Dobson is said to have interviewed serial killer, Ted Bundy, on the last day of his life. In that interview, Bundy is reported to have said that he was raised in a Christian home, but at a young age he was introduced to pornography. Later he began to seek out even more graphic material that connected sex and violence. Eventually, Bundy began to act out these images in real life. We all know the rest of the story.

Do you realize that this stuff all comes from perversions lodged in somebody's mind? Somebody thinks up every nasty picture and every dirty word! What influences their minds to create such images and words? What created and fed these twisted minds that spout this garbage all over our civilization? Who entices the actors and the models? Who takes the pictures and directs the movies? Why are these people so enamored by the easy money for a few hours' work? Because they have allowed themselves to be deceived into being directed by the enemy of all of souls. Now there's a prayer project—praying for the human creators of this evil that Satan is using!

"So, Dad, what do you know about pornography?" More than I want to, and more than enough to be a part of fighting back and helping you do the same thing.

Help From Heaven

A lot of tough situations you find yourself in can seem too big for you to handle. That's true, they almost all are. But they aren't bigger than God; they aren't bigger than the love He'll put into your heart and the power that love packs. How important is your family and your way of life to you?

You have Someone Who can fix it all, and although you may not know Him very well now, you can. The most powerful weapons you can use in this war are a growing relationship with Him and prayer. Maybe you have prayed and you feel nothing has happened. Or maybe things started to look worse once you started praying. Even if things seem worse everywhere you look, God has already begun working. He started answering prayer by placing this book in your hands.

If prayer is one of those things you haven't done in a long while or maybe never at all, you can choose to enter a whole new dimension of life right now. Once you start praying right prayers, things will never be the same again. I will even guarantee that in writing (which I just did!).

The decision you make at this point will define the outcome of your situation. So:

- Do you love your family member who is addicted to porn enough to fight your part of this battle?
- Do you have the patience and desire to take the time necessary to equip yourself with the knowledge and tools you'll need to successfully fight and win your part of this battle?
- Are you willing to commit to this fight even if it means going against your usual way of not wanting to make things worse?
- Are you prepared to do whatever it takes to root out all traces of this evil that has found its way into your family?
- Are you prepared to continue your part of the battle as long as it takes to win it?

Still with me? Then let me ask you this:

- Do you already believe in God and His Son Jesus Christ? If not …
- Do you at least want to believe in God and Jesus, but you've never known how?
- Do you want to be able to trust and believe that with Him as your guiding force, nothing is impossible?
- Do you want to trust by faith and not by what is seen by the eye?
- Are you willing to learn how to do this?

If you've never taken the time to really think about your beliefs or if God has only been an entity who has lived in the shadows of your life until now, this is as good a time as any to get to know Him. That part is really the easiest. He has always known you even if you never took the time to get to know Him. He's always been nearby even if you have lived your life believing that He didn't exist.

He wants to show you that He does exist and He wants to help. If you're thinking:

• If I've always ignored Him, isn't it hypocritical to run to Him because I can't seem to fix this myself?
• I've never done a godly thing in my life, so why should He help me now?
• He'll never forgive me for the things I've done.

Know this! He has been waiting a long time for you to realize that you need Him. He has been standing on the sidelines of your life all this time waiting until you found yourself in a situation that you finally admitted you could not fix without Him. He has waited all his time for you, and He's ready for action now if you're ready to turn to Him.

Starting Your Spiritual Journey

A spiritual journey is really no different than any other where we often start out with a suitcase stuffed full of junk that we don't need. In this journey, you have a suitcase that is filled with junk that not only won't help you; it will actually hinder you. Open up your suitcase and get ready to get rid of some of its useless junk. First toss out guilt and the remorse that always accompanies it.

Close your eyes and tell God you want to get rid of your spiritual baggage, including the belief that you're just getting what you deserve. Ask Him to forgive you for anything and everything you've done that you didn't clear with Him. Please don't go any further until you do it. Did you ask Him to forgive you and really mean it? It's a good idea to do this each and every day or as often as the junk seems to keep resurfacing.

Now, don't keep approaching God with your heart in your hands, saying, "Lord, remember how awful I was to not need you all that time?" Be at peace KNOWING that His response would be very much like this, *"My sweet daughter/ son, I do not know what you are talking about; I cannot recall the time when you didn't need Me."* Once you asked Him to forgive you for those transgressions, He did; then He forgot them. He wiped your slate clean.

"As far as the east is from the west, so far hath he removed our transgressions from us" (Psalm 103:12).

"And they shall teach no more every man his neighbour, and every man his brother, saying, Know the LORD: *for they shall all know me, from the least of them unto the greatest of them, saith the* LORD: *for I will forgive their iniquity, and I will remember their sin no more"* (Jeremiah 31:34).

The situation in which you find yourself has nothing to do with God "paying you back." He loves you, He wants you and those you love set free, and He's not in the business of paying back His sons and daughters! So, let it go. After taking this step of knowing that you need to forgive yourself, the next step might seem a little harder, but it is vital.

Forgiveness of the one or ones who have hurt you is absolutely required for your prayers to be answered from this point forward. God's Word confirms this:

"And forgive us our debts, as we forgive our debtors" (Matthew 6:12).

"And forgive us our sins; for we also forgive every one that is indebted to us. And lead us not into temptation; but deliver us from evil" (Luke 11:4).

He's Forgiven You—Believe It

Since God forgets that your forgiven sin ever happened, it is quite impossible for Him to remember it and resent you for it. You are going to have to learn how to do the same with the person who has betrayed you. Learning to forgive just like God is the secret to cooperating with His miracle answer to everything that is hurting you. Be assured that asking for His help in learning how to do this is almost always necessary in everyone's steps to learning to forgive.

None of us can do this on our own; we have to learn how to let Him teach us how.

So you've asked God into the situation. Good for you! From this point on, stop telling God how big the storm is around you and start telling the storm how big your God is! Visualize that and let it give you the hope it truly contains—God is BIGGER than any ugliness or addiction facing your family!

Remember, you aren't on this journey alone. In addition to your Guide from above in Heaven and Pastor Tom, our spiritual advisor here on earth, I'm also going to introduce you to some ladies and a few men who have come to the *just4ladies.com* community in search of relief and a solution for the same problem with which you are dealing. I am sure their stories will bless and inspire you.

Let's go back momentarily to your suitcase that probably still has a lot of heavy stuff like resentment, despair, anger, and fear. You can get way too involved in tending to the yucky feelings these negative emotions evoke in you. They are guaranteed, if you don't begin removing them, to drain the time you need to focus on the solution to the actual problem that has caused them.

You may find that you hardly ever feel joy, hope or expectation anymore. So, toss out that despair, too, because it's a real time killer. By facing and getting rid of the issues that are making you feel hopeless, you can begin your journey toward the remarkable answers God has for you. It's tough to work toward a miraculous goal when you have so many negative things blocking your view of what's coming up on the horizon.

Despair comes from the combination of all the ugly feelings you are probably feeling right now. Regardless of who in your family may be involved in pornography, despair will be present from time to time. Once you recognize this feeling dragging you down, you can address it and overcome it by following the things you are going to learn as you keep reading.

A lot of people feel ashamed to talk to anyone about the situation that has arisen. That shame or embarrassment can keep you from reaching out for help. You need to start with reaching out to the Lord first because He is bigger than the despair and He already knows the whole situation.

Heavenly Father, I am so grateful that no matter what the situation is in my life, You are here with me. My heart is burdened with the embarrassment and shame of the situation that (Name   )   has fallen into. I know that I can't deal with this problem on my own, but feelings of hopelessness are overwhelming me. Lord, please, help me to feel Your presence in this situation; please fill my heart with hope of the things You are going to do through this situation that will be for good. Father, help me to see past what the world and the flesh sees so that I may rest in the hope that by casting this burden on You everything will turn out all right. Please forgive me for being unable to lean on my faith and trust right now that You will work all things for the good. Help me past the unseen barriers that prevent me from leaning on You right now. Guide me, and I will follow You through these troubled waters with hope, faith, and expectations of the wonderful blessings that You have in store for me and my family. In Jesus' most precious and holy name, I now leave this burden at Your feet. Amen.

A New Way of Thinking

The second step is to change your thinking. Now that you've asked God into this, you have to recondition your thinking to believe and to KNOW that He isn't going to fail you. It would be pretty easy if the feelings of despair would just evaporate and never return, but, for whatever reason, it will take some work on your part to surrender those feelings. God will take them, but He won't pry them away from you. You have to let them go.

"But I just can't help it!" you cry out.

Yes, you can. You have the choice to hang on to the old thoughts and negative emotions that are causing you to feel despair, and one of those old thought patterns has to do with a lack of faith. You can't say you have faith and then not exercise that faith. If you try to mix worry and faith, they are like oil and water. There will always be a mess involved. A good way to start the process of surrendering your way into faith is to confess that you can't fix this situation. Confess that you actually might even make things worse. Confess that God is bigger than your problem. Confess that you can release the "hopeless" into His hands and SIMPLY BELIEVE (that's faith) that He is in control and He isn't going to let you down.

When you think about it, you have nothing to lose and everything to gain. You can hold on to those feelings of despair and go through each day with its crushing weight on your heart and let everything continue to look as hopeless as ever. Or, you can start to think like Jesus. He knew that nothing He faced was bigger than His Father in Heaven. He gave everything—all of it—that He had to face to the Lord and then He never looked back.

What is preventing you from doing the same? Is your answer to that question something like, "I can't SEE anything changing!"? Then pray this prayer:

Lord, I feel so numb right now. I feel like You are not listening. At times I even wonder if You are there. Please help me have faith that You ARE there and that You are helping me regardless of what things look like around me. Help me to have faith that You are working, faith that doesn't depend on what my natural eyes can see. In the name of Jesus, let me feel Your presence and Your peace. Amen.

It's amazing how a simple thought can make you FEEL hopelessness, despair or fear. It is also amazing how a simple prayer can lift that feeling. As you become aware of the things that trigger your bad feelings, begin to declare thoughts of good things to come. I call this believing the miracle to life.

One good example of how to do this is that instead of focusing on your loved one's absence in church, imagine what it will be like when he/she/they return to church or come for the first time. Then take it one step further and place a Bible in their "place" at church and pray a prayer of faith:

"Lord, I know (---name---) isn't here in church today to worship and praise You or to fellowship with other Christians. I know that he or she may be in a place doing things he or she ought not to do. But Father, I am placing this Bible right here (put it right on the pew next to you) *and I am standing in the gap for (---name---) while he or she is away. I am declaring a victory in this war against pornography and by placing* You *(the Word of God) in his or her spot, I am* PREPARING *for the manifestation of this victory!*

Do something every day to declare and prepare for your miracle!

Now that God is your co-pilot, you can get rid of fear using the same steps above. The Bible says in 2 Timothy 1:7, *"God hath not given us the spirit of fear; but of power, and of love, and of a sound mind."* Knowing that fear is NOT from God should make it a little easier to give it to God. Look at it this way: If someone handed you a poisonous snake, would you hang on to it? I didn't think so. Think of fear in the same way; it is poisonous and deadly, so refuse to hold on to it.

Keep getting rid of your baggage and get ready to pick up the weapons He's given you. In just a few more chapters, you can learn how to best utilize the weapons you might not even know that He has blessed you with.

As with everything else in life, you have a choice. You can keep reading or you can put this book down and either go back to trying to fix the situation on your own or you can just give up. I'm hoping you'll keep moving forward with me. Now, there will be times on this journey when you feel like things are going backwards instead of forwards and more than once you might want to give up. Think of what you are getting ready to do—sort of like giving birth. The principle is the same.

Giving Birth

If you're a man, you may need to research these details a little further or you can just take my word for what I'm about to say. But if you're a woman, you'll understand totally (especially if you've given birth). During pregnancy, a woman goes through three trimesters. The first trimester is when her body does all of the necessary changing to accommodate the new life growing inside. Sometimes these changes are uncomfortable, just as change usually is.

In this battle of fighting porn addiction by a loved one, you will find yourself faced with several uncomfortable changes. Sometimes they are painful, they always cause discomfort and some upheaval, and there will be a period of adjustment to the events that are taking place around you.

The second trimester of a pregnancy can start off a little rocky; after all, you're still trying to adjust to all the changes taking place within your body. Then you start getting used to the changes and, in some cases, you find that certain adjustments to them start bringing you comfort. As this second phase progresses in your spiritual journey, you should start to feel peace more often than not as your faith grows and you trust God more easily. You're learning what you can do to bring comfort and peace to yourself and what not to do when these things seem like they are escaping you.

All you moms out there who can laugh at those ridiculous old size five jeans still in your closet can relate to this one. By the third trimester of pregnancy you usually don't remember ever being un-pregnant! Your spiritual journey is similar because by now you still have a day here and there of discomfort, but you've learned to trust God and you pass on through the discomfort. You find that you're pretty content as you bask in His love and grace. You finally believe, without a doubt, that God is on the job and your miracle is in the making.

Then comes the birth. The guys will probably never understand this one, so just go with me on this. Birthing a miracle is almost like birthing a baby. Every time I have ever prayed huge prayers that required huge answers, I have gone through a miracle "birthing process." Have you ever heard of "PUSH" (Pray Until Something Happens)? Many of the women I have coached have reported going through this "miracle birthing" process right before their answers came. It feels like you are in spiritual labor with an overwhelming urge to pray and pray and pray.

This part of the "birthing" process is probably the most intense of all, but even though it is the most intense, remember that it is the final part of the process. The good thing is that it usually doesn't last too long. When it's all said and done and the answer arrives, you can look back and honestly admit that the tough times are hard to remember, the special intimate times spent growing in the Lord will be missed and longed for, and the answer is worth all of it!

Everyone is Going to Have to Change

Somewhere along the line we came to believe and expect that when we look up and pray a prayer asking God for instant intervention, the earth should shake, the mountains should run and—POOF!—the answer should appear out of nowhere. I won't lie to you, when I pray I hope for that response, too. However, I rarely get such instant answers when the problem requires time to fix.

In his book, [3] *Intercessory Prayer*, author Dutch Sheets says that we pray and expect microwave answers to our prayers when in reality God knows that the answer usually needs to marinate for a while. Everyone knows a good steak is better marinated than microwaved, unless you're my kids and have no problem eating a piece of shoe leather if it has enough A-1 sauce slathered on it (*Intercessory Prayer* by Dutch Sheets. Regal Books 1996).

The point is, God *can* snap His divine fingers and make things happen in an instant. But understand this, for you will need to think on this point often in the days or weeks ahead: God not only has to change you to receive the answer, He also has to change the one you're praying for. Give Him a break and let Him rearrange some beliefs and attitudes on both sides so as not to give either one of you spiritual whiplash!

You'll spend time changing and adjusting to the change. You may experience some periods of feeling really yucky and then you'll enter a place of peace and contentment. You may start to feel a little pain again, but you'll find that this time the pain will be accompanied by hope and expectation. Although the labor is a lot of work, you'll soon realize that what you're doing is birthing a miracle.

Miracle birthing can be painful and it is, without a doubt, hard work. But the results are so rewarding. When this miracle is born, you will find that you are a totally different person and your relationship with God and your family member has been renewed, too. You don't want to go back to the way things were even though that may have been your wish for a long time. What you need now is a fresh start.

Although you may not feel that you can function normally each day as you drag your heart around, begin to be open to reconditioning and changing the way you think. You have asked the Creator of Heaven and Earth into this situation. He is very much in favor of families being healed and marriages being forever. You may not know it, but you are in a win-win situation.

So get off that sofa, put the chocolate bonbons away, wash your hair or, at the very least, brush it. That "egg beater" look really isn't you! All good pity parties must come to an end and this is the official end of yours. You have a family to fight for!

3

What Are Today's Kids Thinking?

Victoria's Secret is Really Soft Porn

Let's fast forward now to my life with my kids as they began to reach the age where pornography was coming into my home and I began to realize that things were coming home to roost—ugly chickens with tiny waists and big breasts!

My eleven-year-old son was watching Cartoon Network not too long ago when I went into his room to put his laundry away. I happened to glance at the cartoon he was watching and was shocked to see a cartoon character girl with long sexy legs, a tiny waist, long blonde hair, and breasts that you would normally see in *Playboy* centerfolds. The sounds she was making during her struggle to overcome evil forces were obscene. This was a cartoon character!

"Louie, *what* are you watching?" I shrieked.

"It's *Sailor Moon*, Mom. It's just a Japanese *Anime* cartoon."

"Is this on regular television on a regular channel?" I asked.

"It's just the Cartoon Network, Ma."

Whatever happened to *Tom and Jerry* or *Heckle and Jeckle*? I sat and watched the cartoon for several minutes and then told him to switch it off. He had a fit, of course, but the audio and visuals were obscene. Apparently Japanese *Anime* is one of the hottest types of cartoons around. My teen daughter informed me that it is all the rave among her friends. Most of the *Anime* cartoons I saw were drawn the same way: sexy young girls with high-pitched voices. For crying out loud, the characters were even French kissing in the cartoon!!

This was just the start of my eyes being opened to what our children are now being exposed to. The pornography industry is an approximately twelve-billion-dollars-a-year industry today that doesn't just target men as was once believed. It is targeting our children in record numbers. According to research done by *Family Safe Media*, the largest group of viewers of Internet pornography is kids between the ages of twelve and seventeen. Websites that are supposedly built for "adult entertainment" are being viewed by children!

Built for adults, used by children—what's wrong with this picture?

How are they gaining access to this stuff? Aren't these sites supposed to verify age before they let people view them? The answer is yes, they are supposed to. However, according to *A Survey of Adult Web Servers* of the over two-hundred-ninety-seven MILLION porn links available, only about three percent require age verification. For the most part, all a kid needs to view porn is the credit card that he sneaks out of his parent's billfold and he's in just like that.

But having a computer and Internet access isn't necessary for our children or our families to be exposed to the sexual flavor of the month. Take a look at any *Calvin Klein* or *Gap* advertisement. What do you see? You usually see young girls and guys clad in garments that barely cover their bodies. You will see jeans shorts cut so high they reveal their bottoms or low-cut jeans that actually show parts of the body we're embarrassed to show even our doctors.

Walking past a *Victoria's Secret* store in a mall is like walking past a burlesque club on Bourbon Street in New Orleans. Heaven help us, our teen girls eagerly want the sexy lace undies and push-up bras they see plastered on

Victoria's eight-foot posters in the front windows of every mall. A picture of a model in a lace thong in a provocative pose for anyone to see isn't out of the question. *Victoria* seems to believe that if you just add a pair of angel wings to the model, everything's okay.

Young boys can stand and fantasize in front of these windows or over the ads in common household magazines. How much influence do you think these ads contribute to the unpleasant truth that teenagers are becoming sexually active at a younger age than ever before?

Young girls' desires to become more like the women they see in these ads prompts them to want to be and do what they aren't mentally and emotionally ready to be or do yet. What these advertisements are saying is, "Look how sexy I look in these clothes. Buy them and you can be sexy, too!"

Few mothers want their little girls to leave the house looking sexy. There is only one purpose for that—to attract the attention of the opposite sex. *Victoria's* "looks" can attract far more than the attention of the opposite sex, however. They can literally put your little girl in the path of extreme harm, all the way from unwanted attention to gang rape.

Visual advertising has a large impact on human behavior because humans will always be affected by what they see. A radio ad about *Victoria's Secret* will sell considerably less than the nearly naked mannequins and the eight-foot posters in their windows. The visuals used in advertising today are subtly and sometimes not so subtly laced with pornographic imagery, and they are having a huge impact on what our young people are thinking about and where they are headed. Advertisers know that sex sells and they are targeting our youth and children for the almighty dollar. The porn industry targets our youth at a staggering rate as well.

Let's Start at the Beginning

We start at the beginning by understanding what our kids are thinking, why they are thinking it, and how we can guide their thinking. We have to start at home. Everything in a child's life starts at home. *Everything.*

Home is where we learn where we come from in terms of our ancestry and family history; it's where we learn traditions and values. Home is the base of all the good things we pass on to our children and hope that someday they will pass them on to their children. Unfortunately, home can also be the base of neglect, abuse, and intolerance which also gets passed on to the children who grow up in that home.

Home should be where the kids ask the difficult questions and get practical, honest answers to the best of their parents' abilities. Unfortunately, because of what parents have learned from how their parents answered, evaded, or ignored the hard questions they asked, many of them end up failing to supply good answers to their own kids. Home is where kids ask the question most parents are ill-prepared for or unwilling to answer honestly and directly: "Where do babies come from and how do they get there?" The answer given to this question impacts both boys' and girls' outlooks on relationships for the rest of their lives.

You don't need to read complicated medical statistics to know that a child who is raised in a home with love, respect, affection, encouragement, firm but loving discipline, and good family values will most likely go on to lead a respectable and productive life. Children who raise themselves in homes where these things are absent will go on to raise children without them as well, and their children will do the same until the cycle is broken. Unless a new and healthy pattern is established, generations of behaviors might have to be reversed and undone.

We only need to look around us to see the results of our society's lack of attention to the family as an important unit with moral values being an integral part of that unit. There is a vast difference in family life now from when those of us who are in our late thirties and early forties were growing up.

In the mid- to late-seventies when I was in grammar school, only one of my classmates lived in a single-parent home. All my other classmates and neighborhood friends lived with both parents, and it seemed that everyone in our neighborhood shared the same or a similar set of rules and values.

We all had to be home at the same time at the dinner table because our families ate together. When it was dinnertime, our mothers stood on the front porch and called our names until we came running, and we had better come running quickly. We were always in sight of our homes or close by because most of us weren't allowed off our own block. That was okay with us because all our friends lived on the same block or just around the corner.

Our parents watched us cross the street, bought us ice cream from Mr. Softee (if we earned it), and sat on the front porch with our friends' parents and neighbors on warm summer evenings. When the street lights came on two blocks down, we knew it was time to make the twenty-second dash from wherever we were to our house before our block's lights came on. There was a stiff penalty for not being home when the street lights came on. Those were the rules and we followed them.

The first "porn" I ever saw was when we sneaked into my best friend Jill's room to look at her single mother's *Frederick's of Hollywood* mail-order catalog. That was hardcore stuff back then, and Jill's house was the only place to view it because her mom hardly ever seemed to be home. She was either working or out with her boyfriend.

When we were eleven, Jill spent the night at my house one summer evening, and for the first time in my young life, the subject of sex was discussed in hushed whispers in the dark. We felt we were talking about the real thing, too, like French kissing and "boobs." That was pretty heavy stuff for me. I couldn't begin to comprehend the things she told me she saw her mom doing on the couch with her boyfriend one evening when she sneaked to look. I didn't tell Jill this at the time, but I thought it was kind of gross.

My family, on the other hand, lived in a modest home on the corner; my father owned a construction company, and my mother stayed home and took care of us. As with all my friends, save Jill perhaps, we grew up with traditions and values and life was pretty good. My mom and I disagreed about everything as most mothers and daughters do during the pre-teen and teen years. My dad was my hero and my best friend.

In my family, when one hurt, we all hurt. When one rejoiced, we all rejoiced, and a celebration wasn't complete unless everyone was there. I can still remember my First Holy Communion when my father threw a celebration party the likes of a princess wedding with over a hundred people present. Many years later when I married my first husband, my father gave me a spectacular wedding. Families made memories back then and although it wasn't the fifties, it now seems to have been pretty darn close to that same way of life.

But even then, little by little, society was starting to get lax when it came to family values. The devil saw his opportunity and had already begun stepping through the screen doors of our lives.

My best friend Jill and I lost touch when my family moved to Florida in 1981. I later saw her on a return trip home when I was eighteen. She was a single mom with two young children and stuck in the same cycle her mother had been in when we left. The spirit of fun and mischief that had been in her eyes as a child was gone, and I saw only a sorrow I didn't yet understand. Jill's mother never found the time to teach her the values she desperately needed to know when we were still playing with Barbie dolls on the front porch. She went on to learn about life the hard way.

It all starts at home.

Walking a Week in Their Shoes

Take one week to look at life through your child's eyes. Seriously, for one week don't complain about their music or their friends; and even if it kills you, tolerate their choice of clothes (up to a point). Get a good dose of what they are exposed to and find out more about what is influencing them. Watch the same television programs, listen to their music, and read their books and magazines. Be prepared for an eye-opening (and maybe eardrum-piercing) experience.

A lot of parents would question why they should do this, saying, "I can't control what my kid thinks!" No, you can't, but you can control much of what they are exposed to that will influence their thoughts. This starts at home. Since our focus is on porn-proofing your home, let's start with the most powerful component the porn industries use.

Visuals

While you're "walking out the week," make note of the things that visually stand out the most to you. For example, not too long ago my sixteen-year-old daughter, Ashley, started having some trouble sleeping. I was concerned and after drilling her for any underlying problems she might have been experiencing at school, I switched gears to what she was watching on television before she fell asleep.

Bingo! She had been watching horror films. A lot of teens, myself included back in my day, have an unnerving fascination with horror flicks. Thankfully I eventually grew up and decided that I didn't want anything to do with them anymore. In reality, the movies had started to stress me out.

I don't remember which movie I watched that was the turning point for me, but I do remember it had something to do with a bunch of teens who were trapped overnight in an evil haunted house. Even though this movie was made over twenty years before the special effects were what they are now, the scenes in that movie still stick with me to this day.

I can remember sleeping with my grandmother that night because the movie had scared me so badly.

I still hate to stay home alone at night and I hate the dark. If I'm alone at night, I lie awake with every light in the house on as well as the television. I believe it all stems from that one movie. The visuals that I watched in that movie as a teenager had an influence on me that has infiltrated even my adult life.

Ashley had been watching horror movies with her sister before she fell asleep, which caused the nightmares that kept her awake and prevented her from falling asleep. As soon as I realized that this was the problem, I took action and restricted her from watching any creepy movies at all.

She insisted it wasn't the movies, but I explained that the horror movies were not promoting anything good or wholesome or even educational for that matter. They were simply inviting evil into our home and into her thoughts just before she fell asleep. I asked her to tell me one positive thing she saw in the movies. She couldn't, and she finally admitted that they contained nothing but blood, gore, violence, evil, and, in many cases, sex.

I told her to fall asleep talking to Jesus each night, and He would calm her spirit and fill her head and heart with good and peaceful things. This advice influenced her, even though she is still unable to sleep unless her television is playing. However, she now tunes in to a Christian channel and listens to the music as she drifts off. She hasn't had the nightmares since and sleeps much better.

Influence works both ways. We need to inject as much positive influence into their lives as possible so that it overpowers the negative influences they are exposed to out in the world every day.

Things Aren't Always What They Seem to Be Online

Just because a site on the Internet says that it's safe for children doesn't mean it is. My children were members of

KiddoNet when it first opened, but it wasn't long that I started hearing stories about grown men posing as children on *KiddoNet* and other websites for kids to try to lure them into their traps.

How do you know the new friend your kid made online isn't a pedophile posing as another kid? How do you know that his conversation isn't coaxing your child's personal information out of him in such a subtle manner that even you would have a hard time recognizing it? You don't! The best attitude to have when our kids are involved is that NO ONE is to be trusted online. NO ONE! The price our children can end up paying is too high to take that chance.

As their parent, you have to take the preventive measures necessary to protect them. We're going to cover these measures further on in this book, but there are no easy options and no multiple-choice remedies. If child pornography is generating three to twelve billion dollars per year, that's a lot of people searching for little kids online.

You are responsible for the safety of your kids while they are online.

4

How to Protect Your Daughters While Understanding Their Dilemmas

Dealing with Your Daughters

As I was writing this, my thirteen-year-old daughter, Cassie, came into the kitchen and started the conversation with "Mommm?" That gave me a clue that we weren't going to talk about homework. "You know my friend, Jeanie (not her real name), that we drive home from cheerleading?"

"Well, I drive her so I must know her, Cass," I replied.

"Mom, she told me today that she's pregnant," Cassie said quietly.

"She's WHAT?" I couldn't believe my ears. Jeanie is thirteen years old with the body of an eight-year old. She isn't overdeveloped, covered in makeup, or dressing like she is older—she is just a little kid. She is a child who looks and speaks like a child.

"She's pregnant, Mom," Cassie said again.

"Where are her mother and father?" I asked.

"They're divorced. Her mother is in jail in Florida and she lives with her dad."

I had found it strange when I went to pick my daughter up from cheerleading several times that Jeanie had no ride home. She lives close to our house so I often drove her home. More than once when we pulled up to her home, a gruff, bearded man came out of a trailer and said something like, "I just woke up and remembered I was supposed to come get you."

Cassie said that Jeanie told her she had been having sex with her neighbor. Cassie hadn't believed Jeanie when she told her she was pregnant, but when they went on a field trip together to an adventure park, she believed her. "Mom, she was sick to her stomach all day and couldn't do any of the rides," Cassie said.

How do you keep family traditions and old-fashioned values alive when the kids around your kids are getting pregnant at thirteen? How do you make them understand that this has a lot to do with why you have rules for them that their friends don't have to follow? The answers to those questions are that you do it:

1. Thoroughly
2. Lovingly
3. Firmly

The bottom line is, kids are not only thinking about sex at a much earlier age, they are sexually active at a much earlier age. Why are they thinking about sex before they even hit puberty? Because they are exposed to it constantly on television in the home, from their peers at school, on the Internet, in movie theatres, in the malls, in magazines and books marketed for their age level, in music videos, in video games, and on and on.

The barriers we have to build around our family no longer consist of just simple restriction from certain friends, events, music, or entertainment. The barriers now have to involve almost every aspect of our family's daily lives. Even something as innocent as giving your young daughter a mobile phone is a double-edged sword. Yet, even though I would like to, I don't believe it's healthy or productive to try to isolate them from the world completely. Some day they are going to jump from the nest into the real world and hopefully they'll be prepared and equipped to deal with it successfully.

Focusing In on What's Focusing Them

Understanding how our children think is probably one of the most difficult things we have to do. Outside of your home, your daughter's thoughts are influenced primarily by her peers and the music she listens to. Secondly, her thoughts are influenced by the visuals she is exposed to day in and day out on television, in movies, in video games, and even in print and advertisements.

With the focus of everything that they are being exposed to daily almost always being on sex, it's safe to say that they're probably spending a lot of time thinking about sex, the opposite sex, and how to combine the two. They're also spending a lot of time talking about sex with their friends and unfortunately, the "birds and bees" lesson you have given them or will be giving them will most likely contradict with what their friends swear is the way it really is.

Pornography is all over the place today. Buying a pair of sneakers will usually involve a half-clad woman bending over with her cleavage exposed enticing the potential customer (usually younger people) to buy the brand she's marketing. Or, it will involve a sweaty, heavily muscled, three-quarters naked athlete in a sexy pose. Take a walk through any mall and look at the window dressing, the posters, and the pictures of this sex-saturated marketing.

The pop singers are baring their bellies (and more) and our kids are absorbing it like sponges. We wonder why our kids are so out of tune with what's going on in the family or around them when they spend the majority of their time with an MP3 player plugged into their ears listening to the violent, sexual music that makes up a big part of musical choices of young people today. Pull the plug and limit how much time they spend with the iPod screaming in their ears! Log on to iTunes and click on to some of the "Best Selling"

CD's. Many of them have warnings of "Explicit" lyrics, something that was unheard of fifteen years ago!

Thirteen-year-old girls are no longer interested in a day of Barbie fun; instead they are hitting the movies and even school halls dressed like twenty-one-year-olds on the prowl for their next male conquest. What is influencing this type of behavior in girls so young? Their behavior is greatly influenced by the subtle forms of pornography used in media and marketing all around them!

The pervasive soft-core pornography in magazines, television, advertising, online, and in books provides an illusion for your daughters that is intended to arouse sexual excitement. Allow a young girl who is starting to enjoy the attention she's receiving from boys the opportunity to see physical contact between "actors" on the television, in videos, or in movies, and she will misinterpret it for love. She's going to figure out a way to have that love, too— especially when the boy she has a crush on tells her, "If you love me, you will …" It works in the movies!

Since the beginning of time it seems that women have always been more interested in the emotional aspects of a relationship. This explains the willingness of a girl to sometimes do "whatever." She believes that if she does, then he will have to love her. Girls want love, affection, cuddling, and adoring attention. They want to talk on the phone for hours about their feelings, and they want to hold hands and snuggle and kiss. If you're a woman reading this, can you deny that's what you wanted from your high school beau?

When a teenage girl is so hungry for "love" that she'll resort to giving herself to a boy who claims she will prove her love to him if she does, there is definitely something missing at home. With no guidance or instruction from her home base to understand the feelings she is feeling, she will automatically assume that the boy really does love her. Her heart is full of butterflies and you can almost see those little hearts circling her head. She walks around the house in a daze and will physically attack anyone who answers the phone before she does.

Her thoughts are on the future and where she and "wonder boy" will be. She is mentally picking out curtains and planning a wedding because he has told her that he loves her. Who cares if he's only fourteen; if he makes her feel this good, it has to be love. When wonder boy enters her life, even her friends take a back seat. All she knows is that he's showing her attention, and her hormones are responding.

She turns her favorite radio station on, and she hears all about love, making love, how guys like big "booties" (that means butt ... I have teens, remember?). In music videos, she sees how the girl singing the song hypnotizes the boys with her skimpily clad body and her dance moves. The music videos of these songs can make the lyrics seem tame. Have you seen any of these visuals of young, tight-bodied, short-skirt-wearing girls shaking their "booties?" Gimme a break!

On the flip side, her wonder boy is watching the same thing, listening to the same songs, and getting the same impression of how a girl should act, what she should wear to look sexy, and how she should talk. Marketing companies know this because they have exhaustively researched their target market's thinking. As a parent, it's imperative that you do, too.

Anyone can read this book and follow the suggested steps. Successful results from these steps will require consistent effort and a united parental front (if you are fortunate to be half of a two-parent home). If Mom is opposed to her daughter being exposed to this sexually explicit material and Dad is saying, "Let her have a little fun," it becomes harder for you to fight this war for your daughter.

You Really Were Right, Mom!

How many times can you remember telling your parents, "But my friends are allowed to do it!"? Or that all-time classic, "So and so's mom lets *her* watch those movies!" I know my mother is going to rip this page out of the book and frame it for one of those "I told you so" moments. She'll be right; she did tell me so and since I am at it, I might as well make this page worth framing.

"You were right, Mom."

There are days when I truly wonder why my parents spent money educating me when they knew I was going to have teenagers one day who would know it all. It is these same days that I fully understand why some mother animals eat their young.

The very first step to dealing with your daughters is to sit down and map out a game plan or better yet, a war strategy. This is a battle for your baby girls.

Priorities, Priorities

In a lot of cases, children spend more time under the influence of their friends than they do with their parents. If this is the case with your children, change it. Nothing is more important than your kids. Not your job, extended family, charity work, chores, and even over-extending yourself at church. I'm not saying to quit church, but Pastor Tom wants to come in here:

Note from Pastor Tom: How many preachers and deacons do you know who have lost their families while trying to build a "big work" for the Lord? I'm serious! Preachers and religious workers are losing their families right and left, and I just have to wonder if it is because these people are so very busy doing God's "big work."

That's not the only reason, of course. The devil works extra hard to destroy the families of religious leaders so they will lose their influence in leading others in this very important arena. I came to grips with this many years ago;

and I'm thankful to Dr. Paul Martin of the Psychology Department of *Tennessee Temple College* for making sure I had it correct.

The greatest thing I can give to my children (and now my grandchildren) is to SHOW them that I'm madly, head-over-heels, crazy in love with their mother (my grandchildren's Nana). God originated love, marriage, and the family unit before He established the Church.

The priority of things should be:

1. God
2. Family
3. Church
4. Hobbies and everything else

In my case, God and Church overlap somewhat. My wife, Miss 'Nita, is a totally understanding pastor's wife. There are times that I leave her sick to go visit people who are sometimes less sick than she is. But I don't ever want my kids feeling that they take a back seat to my work for the Church. I do not want them to feel they need to fight the work of God for my attention!

I thank God for all the volunteers we have around our Church. We have a worldwide prayer and preaching ministry; frankly, it would not get done without our core of faithful volunteer workers. But because I want my people to have strong Christian homes, I urge balance with a firm grip on family priorities.

We can get so caught up in an effort to be good Christians who participate and volunteer whenever and wherever needed that we may fail to realize we are neglecting our kids. If we don't recognize that, something is out of whack in our priorities. Church is a vital part of our Christian experience, but it should not take so much of our time that our family loses out. Actually, anything you're doing in excess that takes away from your family isn't healthy for them or for you. This goes for you and your spouse. The key here is balance, a balance that pleases God.

If you're a single parent, keep reading and placing yourself into the instructions that I sometimes label as "you and your spouse." I do understand your situation because I was a single mom for seven years. In other words—been there, done that! Everything I'm writing is doable for a single parent as well and you have your own chapter coming up.

Your Daughter's Friends

Next to the sexual visuals that are sometimes unavoidable, you also have to contend with your daughter's friends who are unavoidable. That some of these friends may come from homes that give dysfunction a new meaning is a fact that can totally escape your daughter's attention. In some cases, negligent parenting can even seem to add credibility to their friends' knowledge because, after all, their friends don't have a wicked mom or dad preventing them from exploring all these super cool things.

One good thing you can do here is pray for your daughter's friends and their families, giving your prayers for your daughter a *ripple* effect. Here is one idea for how to pray ripple prayers:

Lord, I want to bring my daughter's friends to you right now. Some of them are growing up way too fast and I'm afraid that no one, especially their parents, are praying for them. Please hold on tight to these young girls and boys. I ask that You pour out Your love, grace, and mercy upon these young kids who seem bent on trying to grow up so fast. Protect them, place good influences around them, and keep them from bad influences. In Jesus' name, Amen.

I am fortunate now in dealing with my kids' teenage years because my husband will take the lead when I'm too emotional to deal with some of the stuff they bring home. I am getting better, but after nearly thirty years of serving in law enforcement, Mike seems to have a better attitude about hearing problems through without exploding. He knows how to respond without acting purely on the emotions that may or may not be flowing. The kids know which issues to bring to him first. After he's defused the situation, then we all talk about how to best deal with it.

If you don't have this luxury of opting out of the conflict until it's defused because you are the only parent in the home, then you will have to work a little harder to rein in your emotional reactions to your daughter's actions and behaviors. That can be difficult, but God can help you. Either way, single-parent home or two-parent home, here is a prayer that will help prepare you to be Mother Cool!

Dear Lord, I thank You for the gift of my children and for entrusting these precious souls to me to raise and care for. Father, the world is so full of influences that make my job seem impossible at times; I sometimes feel like I am fighting a losing battle. Please, Father, forgive me for losing my patience with them; help me to understand the pressures they are dealing with that I may be a better parent who will meet their needs and yet protect them from the evil they are surrounded by. Lord, I pray for Your clear guidance and strength to stand my ground when it comes to the issues my children bring home each day. Help me to be alert to all of the dangers they face and to never allow exhaustion or the enemy's lies of being defeated to cause me to just give up. Help me to act or not act according to Your perfect will for them and for me. Help me to guide them through these turbulent waters around the actions their friends are taking and, please, bless them with friends who are godly and come from Christian families who will be a good influence on them. In Jesus' precious name I pray. Amen.

Just How Gross Are the Things Our Kids Are Being Exposed To?

Recently my oldest daughter, Ashley, came home and told me about overhearing a group of girls in one of her classes talking about things they had done over the weekend with their boyfriends. These girls were between fifteen and seventeen years of age. Brace yourself, because what I'm about to tell you is shocking!

One of the girls bragged about watching adult videos with her boyfriend and then taking a shower with him afterwards. Apparently one of the features in this adult movie influenced this young couple to try the same thing. The scene she described involved her boyfriend urinating on her because he liked watching that in the movie. The other girls thought it was gross, but she went on to tell them that she is soooo in love with him that she'd do anything for him.

I know my mom isn't going to hang this page on the wall!

These are young teen girls we're talking about, not twenty- or thirty-year-old call girls! These are kids in high school—tenth grade to be exact. My initial response was outrage at the parents of this young and no-longer-innocent girl. My daughter was taken aback by my outburst but once I calmed down, I re-initiated our lines of communication. Then I sat her down with Mike to discuss the issue further. He struggled to hide his shock at what she told him. He has been a cop for twenty-eight years and had not come across some of the situations we were dealing with.

I apologized to Ash for freaking out. Knowing how I am, she said, "That's okay, Mom, I knew you'd freak. But I wanted to tell you about it. Why would someone do something like that?" Mike was out of his league with this issue so he just stood by for moral support.

Ashley and I discussed why her schoolmates are allowing themselves to get involved with the things she is hearing about. She is basically living a "sheltered life" compared to some of these kids. When she displays shock at their stories, they make fun of her. It happens to all kids. My disgraceful experience in the adult-design industry was about to come in handy—at least in the mind of one young girl who I now believe will go on to stand up for her beliefs and maybe influence another person's beliefs.

I spoke to Ashley about the effects adult movies have on people in general, not just young people. For whatever reason, humans are stimulated by watching the act of sex. I used to think that most people could say that about just a normal couple having sex on camera. Nowadays it isn't that simple. The human mind has come up with more perversions than can be written about.

I explained that the things she and other kids *see* will affect how they *feel*, but the important thing is how they *act* upon the visual influence these things have on them. We also talked about how some of those movies are made to "look" like people are really "doing it" and how some of the stuff is merely "smoke and mirrors."

We then moved into the most important part which was avoiding the situations that put her in a position of having to decide whether she might act on her hormones or not. Saying "NO" isn't always easy, but avoiding the situation altogether releases you from a lot of pressure over having to decide what to do. God forbid that our daughters find themselves in a situation where the boy won't take "no" for an answer. Then what?

Moms, You Have a Lot of Experience in Being a Daughter

Most of us, if not all women, already have the experience we need to deal with our daughters. We were their age once and we know what went on in our minds and behind our parents' backs. If we take a moment, we can even remember how we felt and thought about certain boys. The reality of it is that aside from a different wardrobe, better music, and different hairstyles, the principles and situations are exactly the same.

If you are trying to forget some of the things you did when you were young, don't! Let the reminders of your actions and the consequences that followed be the things to drive you to try to keep your children from making the same stupid mistakes. Let your past mistakes prevent them from a future of regret.

If your daughters accuse you of being ancient or of growing up in the "olden days," tell them the same thing: you might have had different hair and different clothes, but you had the same feelings and thoughts. They can't argue with this point and if they do, clarify it. Sometimes they need a firm point driven home. One good response is: "Hormones weren't invented when you were born. Hormones have been around a long time doing the same thing, causing the same feelings and desires in young people since the beginning of time." Period.

Dinnertime Deprogramming for Daughters

Deprogramming your daughters from what the world's visuals are communicating and what their friends are saying has to be a daily event. A good time to do this is at dinnertime. By identifying what porn means and the broad range of things that porn affects and is enmeshed with, you give them the opportunity to look through your eyes.

First, listen to what they have to say and take it from there. If you're up on the latest trends, music, events, etc., it might be easier for you to discuss the issues with your kids. All these things might not have anything thing to do with sex or pornography, but they establish a relevant line of communication with them. As time passes, your daughters will get comfortable talking to you about other things so that when the subject of sex arises, they'll feel more comfortable with asking you questions or telling you what they've heard.

Sometimes, you will have to be the one to bring it up. A good way to do this is to wait for a commercial or some visual with sexual overtones to appear on the television. You can start off by saying, "What does a picture or scene like that make you think about?" Be the first to break the ice because sometimes they are embarrassed to speak about sex with you.

Ask your daughters why they think the girls in those ads dress the way they do. Be point-blank and flat-out ask them if they think the style turns boys on or makes the boys pay more attention to them. It's a good way to get them talking.

Much of what I share with you isn't broken down in scientific data format. But reading and researching data on this issue and then writing about it doesn't even come close to facing a young person and talking with them about it. I have the utmost respect for the experts and their opinions, but I often wonder after reading some of their material if they even have kids.

Believe it or not, I speak to my kids about a sex-related topic at least once a week. I don't mean the details of the "birds and bees"; we did that already. We talk about why I won't let the girls go out wearing certain clothes. We talk about the reasons for wearing those styles and what kind of thoughts the boys may get if the girls leave the house dressed in next to nothing.

Getting Past the Awkward Part to Talking about Relationship

Once we get past the initial awkwardness, we can get into quality conversation about the most important aspect of sex: relationship. With girls, this is really the part they're searching for to begin with. I knew very few girls growing up who wanted to have sex just to have sex. They ALL wanted love and a relationship. That was the goal of whatever they chose to do.

Here's where influence is crucial. Being buddies with your tweens and teens is good, but being a parent who knows what she's talking about is much, much better. You might be an old-fashioned nerd, but little by little as your daughters see your words of warning about consequences beginning to actually happen to their "friends" (the same ones who claim to be the "do all, know all" of human sexuality), the seed has been planted in the back of their mind: "Hmmm ... maybe my mom was right."

The next time they're at school huddled in the lavatory, they may even speak up and voice their opinion. Don't expect them to do it in front of you because that would mean they'd have to admit you might know what you are talking about. Take it back to when you were their age and remember how you so totally disdained what your mother kept trying to tell you, even if you did wonder if there was any truth to it. The principles are still the same.

Teaching Your Daughters about Respect

Looking around us, we can see that so few girls are being taught to be young ladies today. Moms are forgetting to teach their daughters about respect and that they have a right to receive respect from their friends and especially from boys.

I can remember a time when elders were respected whether you liked them or not. It was unheard of for a kid to call someone older by their first name. We didn't drive down the street and scream obscenities out of the car window or whistle and yell out to boys. Today young people will rudely push their way in front of you with their hip-hugger jeans on, butt-cracks in full view, bellies hanging out, and give you dirty looks as they pass as if you had no right to be there.

Without a doubt, self-respect has to start at home. The old adage that parents try to run on their kids sometimes, "Do as I say, not as I do," does NOT work. Kids are going to do what they see. *Visuals*, remember?

If parents are uppity and rude, the kids will be too. Guaranteed. If you're watching movies that are smattered with sex scenes, violence, and bad language, the kids will think it's okay. Guaranteed. A friend of mine told me about a movie trailer (PG-13) she had recently seen on television (prior to prime time!) that had the mother saying to her teenage daughter, "When you dress like that, you look like someone who's looking for trouble." Her daughter's reply was that *was* exactly what she was looking for. Great role modeling for our daughters right in our own homes!

If Mom allows herself to be treated disrespectfully, her daughters are going to think it's okay to be treated that way too. I can write a whole book on this topic alone, and I haven't even gotten into the "boy" part yet!

If your kids are lucky enough to be part of a big, loving, extended family, spend time sharing memories of the past with them. Talk to them about the traditions you would like to see them pass on to their children. Letting our little ladies know how important this is will eventually override what they think is "cool" about not having parents who subject them to rules. It works. My own daughters don't just listen to me talk about family traditions anymore; they bring them up! They've grown to love hearing the "old stories" and are eager to share in these traditions.

School-Clothes Shopping with Daughters— Do I Have To?

My oldest daughter and I could never go school-clothes shopping together. It was a fight waiting to happen from the time we left the house, so Michael used to take her instead. I don't know how he did it, but she always came back with acceptable clothing. Little by little we talked about why I didn't want her wearing the clothes she was picking out. The first thing out of her mouth was, "All the other kids wear them." I hate that statement!

I made a deal with her. I told her that if she would let me pick just one outfit for her to wear to school and help her do her makeup and hair, that if she was made fun of even once, I would let her pick one outfit on her own (within limits) and I wouldn't object. We shook hands on it and I went shopping.

I have tried to keep up with the trends in teen clothing, so I had a good idea of what I was going to buy. My goal was *young and classy*. For her birthday one week later, I presented my picks to her. She loved them! Then I fixed her hair, helped her apply her makeup properly, and sent her off to school. I waited all day with a knot in my stomach to hear the results.

This is a page she can hang on her wall when she's old enough! I know I'm going to.

Mom was right!

Not only did the kids love her outfit, they wanted to know where she had gotten it so they could go buy one, too. They wanted to know where she learned to do her hair "like that" and raved about how pretty she was with makeup.

I was right, I was right, I was right!

No "butt-cheek pants" (our name for hip huggers) for her! She doesn't go to school sending off a sexy message because I don't allow her to, and because she understands where it leads. The best part of her day (in the OUTFIT I PICKED OUT FOR HER) was when one of the baseball players she had had a crush on took notice of her. She liked him because he doesn't talk dirty, he cares about his grades, and he is going to the university when he graduates. I told my daughters to always pick a man who will go somewhere in life, and I was right then, too!

Nowadays, I go with her to buy clothes and even have her wearing pink. Go figure. The visuals, e.g., the advertisements that try to entice her to want to wear skimpy clothing that bares almost all have no effect on her because she understands now why they're used. Her friends wear butt-cheek pants, but she has been spending more and more time with kids who don't. She has changed her focus from trying to fit in to simply picking a crowd she didn't have to lower her standards for.

It all started at home.

Little Girls Going All The Way

Girls are more willing to "go all the way" than they used to be because in their search for "love" today, they're willing to sacrifice themselves in hopes that the boy will feel the same. These days, kids are going all the way as young as thirteen and fourteen. Just a few decades ago, sex was something you did for the first time with your spouse. If a girl ventured into forbidden waters before she had a wedding ring on her finger and was found out, she was basically "tainted" to the point of never having any hope of finding a decent mate.

Welcome to the new millennium where kids having sex is considered just a way of life. Instead of teaching them to abstain, our schools are handing out condoms claiming that they are trying to prevent unwanted teen pregnancy. One government statistic I remember reading said that the United States has the highest rate of teen pregnancy and births in the western industrialized world. Teen pregnancies are said to cost the United States at least $7 billion annually.

Thirty-four percent of young women become pregnant at least once before they reach the age of twenty—that's about 820,000 a year. Eight out of ten of these teen pregnancies are unintended and 79 percent are to unmarried teens.

I recently read an article in *Seventeen* magazine (May 2006) about a high school in Ohio with a student body of approximately 470 kids. Out of a student body that size, sixty-nine girls were pregnant. That's a lot of teenage mothers in one high school! It's a lot of teenage fathers, too. The impression that I got from the girls being interviewed was that they were only at a loss because the school didn't teach them what to do after they became pregnant.

Schools now offer programs that cater to new "young mothers." All the girls interviewed in the *Seventeen* article agreed that the general consensus at school was that it was very cool to be pregnant. I never thought I would see the day when high school girls would think it "cool" to be pregnant. What is more alarming is that so many high school boys are fathering children by not one girl but multiple girls. What a mess!

The entire article only mentions one girl whose boyfriend was willing to stick by her and marry her when they were able. Another girl went on to report that her boyfriend bailed on her and denied the baby was his. A short time later, she learned he got another girl pregnant. Where are their parents?

When a boy is raised with the wrong belief that they should be allowed to sow their "wild oats," then the parents who agree with this logic had better be prepared to support the end result. It all starts at home.

When parents have the attitude that boys should be able to get away with a little more than girls, they should try being the mother who just found out that her fourteen-year-old daughter is having a baby and the fourteen-year-old father has abandoned her. Sadly, even if the young father sticks by the young mother-to-be, what good will it do? He isn't old enough to legally get a job, and an eighth-grade education (if he has one) doesn't make for a promising future.

Boys who are "getting away with more" because they are boys are at least 50 percent responsible, perhaps more, for the unwanted teen pregnancy rate that is blowing the roof off our nation. They are at least 50 percent responsible for the fact that there are more and more single mothers raising babies while they are still babies themselves. Most of these boys go on with their lives while the young girls struggle to support babies they aren't ready for, or they leave them with their parents to raise.

This is a high price to pay for all involved in the belief that boys should be able to sow a few wild oats before they settle down. This belief is part of the vicious and destructive cycle that is tearing the core of our family values apart. So, let's talk now about dealing with your sons.

5

Understanding and Protecting Your Sons

Little Boys—Little Men

As previously mentioned, research done by *Family Safe Media* shows that the largest group of viewers of Internet pornography is kids between the ages of twelve and seventeen. They go on to report that teenage boys become addicted the fastest. The porn industry knows that marketing to young boys will create a steady stream of income for this multi-billion-dollar industry, and they do not care that these boys will have to deal with the problems that exposure to pornography will cause them for years to come.

As a parent, the discovery of porn in your sons' lives can leave you wondering what you failed to do or not do to ensure that this foreign substance would never invade your family. Questions race through your mind and waves of physical pain can wash over you and settle in your chest. You have just stepped into a full-fledged war for your family and for the life you have worked hard to build.

When little boys reach puberty, somewhere between the ages of nine and fourteen, they need a male role model in their lives to explain what's happening to their bodies and in their thoughts. They need a father figure (preferably right in their own homes, but we know that isn't always going to happen) who is ready to make these little men understand that what their friends at school are saying about girls and what they think they want to do with them is bad news.

Most importantly, young boys need a strong male role model to help them understand how to control the urges they're feeling and what the consequences are for not controlling them. Boys need men to teach them the right and wrong way to treat a woman, and why it's important to wait and not act on the sexual urges they are naturally feeling.

As with our daughters, our sons should have a parent at home when they arrive from school. This can seem to be an almost unsolvable problem for single moms and single dads. I was a single mom for seven years, and I understand the necessity to financially support the children you've been left to rear mostly on your own and in some cases completely on your own.

But I believe that instead of looking at this as an unsolvable problem, you can turn your situation into an opportunity to do great things. I believe it because God helped me manage to do it. I've also coached other single parents, mostly moms, through the often scary steps they needed to take to put their kids first.

Our sons can't raise themselves and we can't allow television and their friends to raise them for us. By leaving them alone for hours each day, that's exactly what we're doing. According to the *A.C. Neilson Company*, parents spend an average of only 3.5 minutes a day in meaningful conversation with their children. Is that enough time for a parent to be a parent? No!

One of the most common responses I hear from my clients is that they are afraid to take a chance on leaving their current job for one that would allow them more time with their kids. They are very fearful of even thinking about trying to work in a home situation. The second most common response I hear is that they "can't afford" to change. You can't afford to lose your sons to the evils of this world, either. Will the security of that job be worth visiting your child someday in a drug rehab, a prison—or worse, a cemetery?

I know that sounds really heavy, but the bottom line is you can make changes and survive financially. You just need to believe that the same divine Helper you've already heard about in previous chapters is with you on this matter as well. As you spend time learning about the Lord, you will learn that His will isn't for families to disintegrate, but it is for them to thrive and maintain the values He set forth for families from the beginning of mankind.

Making Some Scary Moves—You Can Do It!

I would love to tell you that there's a special job section in your local paper that has a listing of perfect positions that will pay you top dollar and allow you to work from home so you can spend time with your kids. But it wouldn't be true if I did. And those hundreds of websites online that offer you too-good-to-be-true job scenarios aren't telling you the truth, either.

The fact of the matter is that you need to take this need to the best Job Recruiter there is! You can take your need right to the Lord! He will help you if you are genuinely serious about wanting to find a solution to being with your kids to protect them.

If your sons are alone for more than an hour in the evening, search your mind to think of any alternatives you can. Perhaps you can pay someone to come in for one or two hours. Perhaps you can leave them with a relative or a trusted neighbor who will enforce similar rules to your own.

If these aren't options for you, then contact your child's guidance counselor and explain the situation and your concerns. Ask if there are other families whose kids attend the same school as your sons who might let them stay with their families for an hour or two until you get home. Most school counselors are willing to try to help you. Check with your pastor or priest and explain your concerns to them. You'll be surprised at how they might be able to help.

You may be even more surprised at the support system you've had around you all along, but that you have been too busy trying to do it on your own to realize it!

At the same time that you are trying to secure a safe environment for your kids, think about the perfect employment situation that would allow you to be there for them and still support them. I'll let you in on a BIG secret: God can bring you to the perfect opportunity or He can bring the perfect opportunity to you! You just have to have an intense desire to put your kids first and protect them.

Dutch Sheets has prophesied that we are now in a time of great creativity, new inventions, new strategies, and more. Ask God to give you an invention or a new strategy for solving some problem that is still being grappled with by the people who grapple with such things. Ask God to show you a need that no one else is filling right now in your area of influence, as well as ideas of how you can fill it with little or no start-up cash or special equipment. Ask God to bring opportunities your way that you can't even imagine. He can and He will if your desire is strong enough and your faith in Him is deep enough.

Let's start with a prayer for help that is backed with the knowing that your desire to protect your children is without a doubt God's will for your situation!

Heavenly Father, I am so very thankful for the blessing of my children and I know that they are a precious gift from heaven. Lord, I want to do everything I can to nurture and protect them. Father, I am in a situation where I believe I have to work to provide the necessities for these children. But I choose to believe that You give each of us our daily bread, so I am ready and willing to let You guide me to the perfect situation that will allow me to raise my kids the way You would have me raise them. Please guide and direct my ambitions and expectations and lead me to the perfect opportunity to receive this blessing. I know this is Your will for my children and me. In Jesus' name, Amen.

Now that you've prayed this prayer, start declaring the victory and begin preparing for the outcome! Let your kids in on your prayer request and expectations and teach them to pray for it also. Before you know it, an answer that you may have never dreamed of might arrive when you least expect it. God will move to provide your answer because of your faith and His will for families. Keep your heart and mind opened to His guidance and direction, knowing that He may lead you down a different and better path than what you may be thinking.

One day boys are playing with their G.I. Joes, skateboarding, and hunting worms; the next day they realize that girls aren't as gross as they once thought they were. Maybe they're even kind of neat. Boys present a whole different set of issues to deal with than girls. Tom has a pretty interesting view on the subject of boys and the opposite sex.

A Note from Tom: I once heard about a conversation that two little kids were having. One said to the other, "Am I the opposite sex, or are you?" The point here is that the term "opposite sex" was an intriguing idea to the little guys. If that conversation leads into trying to find out more sexual information before little Billy is ready to handle it, it could lead to serious consequences.

A healthy attitude towards "the opposite sex" is normal. The Lord created the human body with a sexual drive right there at the start. To sweep it under the rug and assume that sex is inherently "dirty" and unhealthy is wrong because it infers that somehow the Lord made a mistake when He made man and woman attractive to each other. It was no mistake.

If a young boy learns about most of his sexual "education" from pornography, he may forever misunderstand the healthy love that God intended between husband and wife. That misunderstanding from childhood impressions gleaned from pornography, as well as the unwise handling of problems of a sexual nature by unthinking parents, can lead to sexual problems and deviant behavior during his entire adulthood. This leads to and reflects other spiritual problems as well. Sadly, I deal with them far too often.

The Leaders of the Pack—Teaching Boys to Lead

Boys have to be taught to be leaders. The "rule" for so many generations has been that the girl is supposed to say no when it comes to sex. We need to teach our boys the same thing, maybe even more so, because males are supposed to be the leaders, the stronger half of the boy/girl equation. They certainly are half of the equation that creates unwanted teenage pregnancies. They should be learning to lead in a right manner.

Just as a young teenage boy is dealing with raging hormones and a changing body, his friends at school may be claiming to have "gone all the way." They are using words and describing things they supposedly have done with girls. In the past, they were often lying about this; in all probability they may be telling the truth today. Your teenage son may want to try to keep up with what his friends say they are thinking and doing.

Sex trash talk is something all boys do. They think that they and their friends have all of the answers, and they think they know all there is to know about sex. They go to school or out to hang with the guys and come back home programmed with a totally inaccurate picture of what sex is all about. Add to this an Internet connection with access to chat rooms where the naked women are in abundance on their monitors, willing to do whatever they are directed to do so long as the credit card keeps working, and that spells D-I-S-A-S-T-E-R.

Boys hear the graphic stories their friends tell, they watch television programs dripping with sex-studded advertisements every day, and they view movies that should be burned. When they get bored with that, they flip on the Sony PS2 and play violent games like *Resident Evil*, *Grand Theft Auto*, and others that are loaded with female images that are designed to stimulate.

When was the last time you sat down and actually watched the video games your young guys are playing? It's a real eye-opener, let me tell you. "Chicks with guns in tight leather body suits, shooting the crap out of dead people walking," was the way one boy described his favorite PS2 video game. Talk about visuals! Holy Cow! And they haven't even gotten online yet!

Too many parents figure, "Oh well, he's just a kid; let him have his fun while he can." Not good. Boys spend more time watching television, playing video games, and surfing the Net than girls do. The statistics say it is something like an 80 percent versus a 20 percent ratio. I don't need a statistic or a $200-an-hour kiddie shrink to tell me that. I have three kids, and I'm exposed to the stat-making evidence, behaviors, desires, and actions twenty-four hours a day for free.

Trying to deprogram what their friends have told them all day in school is a mountain in itself, but if you allow them access to all these other "fun" things, you're looking at Mount Everest. Such deprogramming and controlling the amount of filth that is probably being viewed in some manner in your home has to be done daily to be effective and produce the results you're aiming for. If you don't, your foothill of sexual interest is going to morph into "Mount Everest."

Ghetto Garbage

Teens' music videos today promote "ghetto" style and attitude where women are not girlfriends; they're "hoes" and "bitches." Then on television, young guys can watch a sexual free-for-all: sex with numerous women with no commitment. You may have to do something really drastic, parents, like putting the source of the filth out of their reach by cutting the cord to the cable!

"What? Get rid of my cable? But I love HBO and *The Sopranos*!" was the response I got from one mom who was asking what she should do about the unhealthy amount of time (an hour or better) her son was spending in the bathroom with the door locked. This young boy has his own television in his room. When this mom received a cable bill with extra pay-per-view charges, she discovered her son had been ordering adult movies in the middle of the night.

He wasn't spending any time outside with his friends, he was on the Internet with his bedroom door locked, and he was playing violent video games. But his mother only became concerned enough to contact me when she found a *Victoria's Secret* catalog under his mattress. What's wrong with this picture, or should I say, these pictures?

Her husband told her to just let him alone because he was only being a "boy." She said her husband told her that he had done it as a kid, and that he still received his monthly *Playboy* which he "refused to give up." He said, "You're just being insecure; all boys do that."

When her son talks about girls, he refers to them as "bitches." When she tried to talk to him about any interest he had in the girls at school, he told her girls are only good for one thing. Everything she did with her son to try to undo his friends' influence or remove the harmful visuals from him, her husband undid or refused to enforce. His father actually made matters worse by making statements like, "Did ya see the rack on that one, son?"

Far too many high school boys today have the same attitude. Do you know why? Because that's what they're allowed to watch and see right in their own homes, and no one is telling them it isn't right and that it needs to stop.

"Some days it feels like it's them against me," she told me. Her son is only fifteen years old, but he already believes that women don't deserve respect. The music videos he keeps on his television all the time depict gangster-like scenes with women dressed in micro-miniskirts hanging all over rap singers with gold teeth, pants that look like Omar the Tent Maker fitted them, and flashing gang signs and insignias.

It's "in" to be a "gangsta" because the visuals they see are taking something evil and romanticizing it with hard-bodied females. The Rolls Royce automobiles, the fear and power that portray the singers' "gangsta" status earn them respect from the community around them. Adding these visuals and fantasies to music videos pumps up the sales of such recordings in a phenomenal way.

Deglamorizing the Ghetto

I had the opportunity to work in a ghetto once where my father owned a building that had belonged to his father. Many decades ago, when the building was bought, the neighborhood was good. When we went back to New York to deal with the property more recently, the neighborhood had deteriorated into a ghetto. Although I did see a few gold teeth and some gold chains, I never saw one of those guys driving a Rolls. Instead, each morning as I arrived, I saw prostitutes and had to chase them away from the corner where our building sat.

Across the street I would watch the drug dealers go in and out of the place which I later found out was where they made the drugs they sold. After seven o'clock at night, my dad forbade me to go outside the door. To use a time-worn cliché, it was a war zone. One evening we were there late and as I was standing in the shop with my dad, we heard noises like firecrackers getting closer and closer. My dad threw me on the floor of the garage and fell down next to me.

There was a drive-by shooting across the street at the drug house. The police removed four bullets from the outside wall of our building alone. Had my dad not reacted as quickly as he did, we could have been shot.

There was nothing romantic about any of this! This was reality, and it was bad! These guys, the real thugs and gangsters, were hardened criminals with no care or concern for anyone. The women I chased away from the corner of our property weren't sexy, foxy young ladies in two-hundred dollar microskirts and Gucci heels; they were girls who sold themselves for their next fix of whatever drug they were addicted to.

My dad couldn't sell that property fast enough. Right before we left for the last time, the DEA, FBI, and local police agencies raided the drug house. It was terrifying, but it also gave me a glimpse into a world that less than one percent of these kids will ever see for what it really is. Maybe God had a reason for my being there for those few short months. It wasn't for the "gangsta" romance, that's for sure.

Boys go to school today and get with their "homies" where they talk about doing things with girls that they see in these outlandish videos. The woman I was coaching told me that her son's favorite song was "I'm in Love with a Stripper" by a rapper called T-Pain. I saw the video online, and it was just as bad as the title and the lyrics of her son's favorite song.

Our kids are products of what they are exposed to. If that exposure isn't at the very least guided, explained, and clarified, then they're going to pick up what their peers share with them. This kind of exposure can be like ignoring unguided missiles coming into your son's mind and your home.

Right now, it's trendy to have a "gangsta" look and a stable of "hos." The slang is vulgar, but it's "in." Amazingly, the girls don't seem to mind playing the part. One of my friends asked her son what he thought was so cool about being a gang member; he told her that all the guys at school were "thugs" and that was cool. These kids wouldn't know the first thing about being a thug and they would probably survive about twelve seconds, if that long, in a real ghetto.

The woman I tried to help received no help from her husband and she refused to take the drastic steps that needed to be taken by removing the elements that were causing the problem. She let things stay as they were. This kid is headed for big trouble. God help the parents whose daughter brings him home. I learned later that this woman herself was and is a victim of abuse, which contributes to her failure to stand up to the father and the son and take necessary action.

These parents are a classic example of how to make a bad situation worse.

Dealing with Boys—the Rebels

I've greeted my husband at the door on more than one occasion and blurted out the words, "Just DEAL with him!" This was when I had had a day where my son had literally pushed me to the breaking point. The only one capable of dealing with him without hurting him, as well as dealing with me for that matter, was Mike. Someone had to be the rational parent! It's not easy dealing with sons; I know!

If your kid has his own television, as many teens do, and you don't want him exposed to adult movies, utilize the parental features on the television to block the channels that show inappropriate movies. If that doesn't work and he finds a way to override it or finds another channel, there's another fail-proof solution. Take the television out of his room! It would be best if you and your husband took a stand together on this, but if there is no father in the house, you have to be the parent.

When you've tried everything else and that hasn't worked, you have to get drastic. Have his father explain, or if you have to, you explain to your son that you know he's starting to hear things from the guys at school about sex. You know that he may even think he's ready to have sex himself, but you don't want him getting his sex education from the guys at school or from the television. Tell him that you totally understand that a major focus in his life right now is sex. Reassure him that he isn't the only boy going through this phase, but that you are determined that he will be one of the few who will get through it with the right views and values. You're the boss; be the parent. Get him to listen to what you have to say. He'll probably get upset, but this is the perfect opportunity to explain to him that the things he sees in those movies are not the way love and sex really are. Explain to him that watching those movies may stimulate him to want to do the things he sees, but that really isn't what sex is all about.

Visual Males and Lustful Thoughts

Males are visual creatures. In their teens, their hormones are driven strictly by visuals. You won't hear about many fourteen-year-old boys falling in love; you will hear plenty about plenty falling in lust, though. That's what it is: lust. Parents, you need to let your son know why it's tragic if he tries to form his insight about sex from someone else's fantasies or from any form of pornography.

Outline the consequences for him of irresponsible sexual activity:

- Unwanted pregnancy that he would be half responsible for.
- Sex with a partner who may have been with numerous others, exposing him to disease.
- Robbing the woman he falls in love with of one of the most special parts of himself—his purity.

Many boys will laugh and roll their eyes. They will say they aren't ready to be worrying about getting married. A great response to this is to remind them if they aren't ready to deal with adult issues such as marriage, sex shouldn't be on their itinerary either. One goes with the other in basic family values.

Deprogramming the boys from the start and not letting up for a day is critical. The effort is extreme, but the end results are a young man who will not look at a woman as an object, but as someone who deserves respect. Besides, "hoes" are supposed to be garden tools!

Back in the days when a guy had to apply a little pressure to a girl to get her to go all the way, he had to promise her the world and the love "word" was absolutely a must. Even if he didn't feel that way, he knew it might get him around the bases. These days, the girls are the aggressors in many cases. Your son may not need to jump the hoops and promise a lifetime commitment, as was the case with past generations. That makes it even easier for him to disrespect the girl and satisfy his urges and his curiosity.

This is where prayer is all you might have to protect your son. Well, know this! Prayer is guaranteed to be the most powerful form of protection you can give him. God can go with him and get through to him where you can't. Keep God in the loop of trying to deal with your sons.

You Have to Step Up to the Plate and Hit the Ball

You don't need to spend hours and hours researching statistics to know that our society has bailed out on our kids. Now more than ever before, it is our job as parents to protect them. Your son's attempts to stay with the crowd mixed together with the soft porn in today's television and movies is like throwing gasoline on a smoldering fire. How convenient it is these days that soft- and even hard-core pornography is just a mouse click away.

The problem with this is twofold. First, boys can easily feed powerful desires that are usually too tough for them to stifle. Second, they are getting an impression of sex from sources that promote JUST sex! There is no respect or love in pornography; the depictions in all their forms are fantasies about the erotic "quickie." There are no love stories or comedies in porn films. There aren't any story lines, and there aren't any Oscar-winning actors or actresses in these films. The films are about sex, period.

With boys, the most important thing you need to do first is remove pornographic material from your home. Get rid of the dirty magazines your husband may have. If your son knows Dad is looking at these things, he's going to think it's okay to look, too. That old line that Dad might use that he buys the magazines just for "the articles" isn't going to cut it. *Visuals*, remember? It's all about the visuals!

Get rid of the novels that you have that are loaded with steamy love scenes and lots of sexual imagery. If Mom enjoys reading erotic writing, young boys and girls will think it is all right to read it, too. Erotic writing can create powerful visuals in the mind because their sole purpose is to sexually stimulate. Root out the calendars that are not appropriate for a child to see—like *Sports Illustrated* Swimsuit Edition or Hooters Girls. Do you think these visuals are innocent because they're just beautiful girls in bikinis? These publications are all about sex. Provocative visuals sell sex!

Many parents laugh at me when I tell them this. The first thing they say is, "Don't you think you're taking it too far?"

My response? "No! I don't!" I have said it before and I'll say it again: what you get out of this war is directly related to the efforts you put into fighting it.

Pastor Tom tells of a little fellow who went to church to hear his dad preach. When they took up the collection, he saw his dad put in a half-dollar. When the church official gave the visiting preacher the offering, it was a half-dollar. As they were getting in their car the little boy said, "You know, Dad, if you had put more in, you would have gotten more out."

It's the same thing here. If you're going to pick and choose what you think is okay and what is pornographic based on how liberal or conservative you are, then you're going to end up with results that go along with those beliefs. Whether you are trying to porn-proof your home for boys or girls, you need to determine that no form of porn, hard or soft, is healthy. No form of it.

On September 27, 1943, *Time* published an article by Indiana University's Psychologist Glenn V. Ramsey (www. time.com/time/archive/preview/0,10987,850358,00.html). He had found that young boys (under fourteen) were most stimulated by talk of sex where older boys were stimulated by seeing naked girls. Next to these were daydreams, obscene pictures, movies, and burlesque. This article was written long before the Internet opened the doors to far worse visuals: higher quality pictures, millions of videos, and a never-ending supply of erotic visuals and literature, live chat, live video chat, and other nasty stuff that will feed a young boy's daydreams to the point where they become uncontrollable.

6

BOLO—Be On the Look Out!

Obvious and Not So Obvious Signs

I've always liked watching any kind of documentary that involves investigations. Mike doesn't like to watch these shows. He claims that when you do it for a living, it's not something you want to come home and watch more of. He gets his fill of investigations on the job. I, on the other hand, love to investigate and analyze everything until I get to the root of the issue or problem.

Some people simply don't know what to look for in order to make sure pornography hasn't gotten into their homes; some don't even realize that it can get into their homes. Whether you're raising girls or boys, there are signs and indicators you can look for and things you can do to take preventative measures.

Here's a few of the obvious signs that pornography in some form may be leaking into your home and family:

Girls: An overnight personality change when it comes to clothing, hair, and makeup is a clue that something is not right. They'll go from being comfortable in their jeans and T-shirts to wanting to dress more provocatively with high heels and tight or revealing outfits. They'll either start wearing makeup or start wearing it heavier to emphasize certain features such as eyes and lips. Hair will go from styles they've always been comfortable with to requests for color changes, highlights, or sexy styles.

Boys: They'll spend more time in their rooms with the door locked. Boys tend to keep their activities in this area very private.

Girls: If you want to know your daughter's deepest secrets, read her notes or diary. I know that some people would disagree and object to this; but as a parent, that's where you'll find everything she's thinking about. You simply have to weigh the consequences of not knowing what she's thinking about against the possibility of saving her from serious consequences of acting on those thoughts. Perhaps you will even find that she's doing fine and you can trust her.

If reading her diary can be done without her knowledge, this is best. If she knows you're reading her most secret and guarded thoughts and actions, she'll stop recording them immediately. Don't let guilt stop you from peeking into her private life. You're the parent, remember? Knowing what she's into makes helping her easier.

Boys: More time than usual being spent on the Internet and a lot of time online late at night or when you're not home. These are the times he can surf without worrying about getting caught.

Girls: Although girls are less likely to become obsessed with hardcore porn like the stuff you'd find on Internet porn websites or in adult magazines, they are likely to go for soft-core versions that are presented as "educational." There are many magazines, websites, books, blogs (online journals), and social communities that offer females tips on being more sexually "desirable."

Let's address these problems from the standpoint of what your kids are being exposed to that will make them not only think about sex, but things that actually are a crossover into becoming sexually active.

BOLO (Be On the Look-Out) for the All-knowing Friends!

First and most powerful are the friends who are influencing your daughter at least five full days each week.

These friends might not have parents who are actively concerned about the porn epidemic, so you may find yourself standing in the gap for them as well as for your daughter. Remember when I mentioned praying with the ripple effect earlier. God won't say, *"Sorry, the time I will allow you to spend praying for young girls is all used up now. Sorry you didn't get to your own daughters yet, but come back next week!"*

God will bless and move in the lives of every young girl you will lift up to Him, coming into agreement with Him that He can fix the brokenness in their lives that no one else seems to know what to do about. He'll also bless you for standing in prayer for kids that no one else is taking a stand for or praying for.

You might have the upper hand with your little girl when she's at home. But then she goes off to school with the belief that the more she can get away with, the cooler she will be in the eyes of her peers. She hears how her friends are "sooo falling in love" and their guys "sooo love them back," and they are going "all the way" and it's "like, totally awesome!" Then comes the dreaded question: "Like, have you done it yet?"

Pow! The pressure is on your little girl to keep up with the crowd. When the young girl she's talking to starts giving her details and telling her how much her boyfriend likes this or that, your daughter is probably trying to maintain her composure and her cool factor. She may even tell her friend she knows all about it, when in reality she probably doesn't know zip! Before you get angry at the hypothetical young girl filling your daughter's ears with this junk, remember the ripple principle of prayer!

So what does your daughter do now? She beelines it home and hops on the Internet and starts her research. She won't have to look far because all she has to type into the search engine is one of the choice words or phrases that her friend used, like "oral sex" or the slang for it (which I won't use because my mother AND my pastor are both reading this book), and voila! Your baby girl has two gazillion pages of reference with illustrations and tips on how to please a man.

Let me repeat that: HOW TO PLEASE A MAN! The Internet has just bumped her up to learning about how to please a man. One thing leads to another, and she's surfing her way to a sexual education you couldn't even begin to explain to her.

Here's what you can do to counter it: Communicate!! Moms, it's time to do what we gals do best! TALK, TALK, TALK! A mom has two extremely important roles in her daughter's life. The first is to nurture, teach, set the boundaries, and basically be a mom. To this day when I am sick, I want my mom. The second role a mom has to play is best friend. Then she has to know how to strike a balance between all these roles. In my house, we have "Mom is cool," but we also have the "Don't cross the line" thing going on.

After one of our discussions about the vulgarity of rap songs and rappers, my girls challenged me to try and make a rap that wasn't vulgar in some way. OH, GIRLS, stand back! This is Mighty Mom you're throwing that challenge down to! I pulled my oversized Sponge Bob jammie pants down to the top of my thighs so that my Felix the Cat undies were visible, like those guys that walk around with their boxers hanging out. I began stomping my pink, fuzzy-slippered foot on the floor and clapping, and I cut loose the rap of the century!

*Bang-Bang-Clap; *Bang-Bang-Clap; (here comes the lyrics)* "My name is MOM!" *Bang-Bang-Clap; *Bang-Bang-Clap;* "I'm the Real McCoy!" *Bang-Bang-Clap; *Bang-Bang-Clap;* "I'm sweeter than" *Bang-Bang-Clap; *Bang-Bang-Clap;* "An Almond Joy!" *Bang-Bang-Clap; *Bang-Bang-Clap.* "Don't touch my daughters!" *Bang-Bang-Clap; *Bang-Bang-Clap;* "If you're a boy!" *Bang-Bang-Clap; *Bang-Bang-Clap.*

Had my daughters not been rolling on the floor laughing hysterically to the point of choking, and had Mike not come upon this scene prematurely, I could have finished. Who knows, I might have started a new trend in music. Sometimes you just have to join the kids in their own games! I pulled my Sponge Bob jammies back up, elegantly lifted my chin and exited the room, having made my point about rap music.

An open line of communication that can be both fun and serious is incredibly valuable. Once they know that you are way cooler than most "old people," they'll open up and start bringing those "pressure issues" to you because they realize everything you've told them has been right. Get to know you're daughters and let them know you. When they ask if "you did this or that" as a kid, be honest. Then share with them the price you had to pay for what you had done.

BOLO (Be On the Look-Out) for Sex in the Marketplace—Buy Cheap for a High Price!

Kids are exposed to an overtly sexual marketplace where the driving force behind the ads is "sex is universal, sex is cheap, and sex sells." These sleaze marketers do everything they can to come as close to the fine line of acceptability as possible to utilize that marketing strategy. The problem is, no amount of money could possibly be worth the real price we pay for their garbage.

Here's how you counter it: The second hardest thing after deprogramming their brains and draining out the junk their friends have filled them with is explaining why the things that are so popular *are* so popular. This can feel like a Porn 101 class in some cases. But it ties in directly with the "friends" issue because those kids' parents let them wear the things that are being peddled through these sexual ads.

Lay it out to your kids the way it is and answer their questions with accurate facts and details so they really have little left to argue about. Point out some obvious facts such as how their friend who is allowed to purchase and wear provocative clothing may already be sexually active. They might argue that this is not the end of the world, maybe even cool in their circle of friends. Counter with the fact that irresponsible sexual activity puts their cool friends in the high risk categories of unwanted pregnancy, sexually transmitted disease, and even sexual assault.

I tried and proved this method and it works every time. Let me take you on a little shopping expedition with the Washam family. Right before school starts, we take one weekend to go shopping for school clothes with our kids. I pack for the trip. First I bring a good book so I have something to read when I storm out of the store in a fit of rage and have to wait on Mike and the girls to finish. Then I bring a snack because, after all, he is shopping with two teenage girls.

I load up on Excedrin and pray for three days prior to the scheduled trip while asking everyone on my prayer list (over a million people) to pray for me also. The night before we plan to go, I avoid all websites that have any reference to mother's doing serious bodily harm to their kids. I focus mainly on websites that explain how to achieve serenity in three steps or less. I then go to sleep and get a good night's rest.

The next morning we go to the mall. Once we arrive, I find myself surrounded by three thousand other parents with the same book in their bag and a "Why do I do this to myself every year?" look on their faces. I do believe that Excedrin does record sales that week.

Upon walking by the *Victoria's Secret* store, my sixteen-year-old daughter spots the girl in the poster with a sheet of crinoline wrapped around her naked body, a pair of angel wings and nothing else, and says, "Oh, Mom! I want that!"

"Ashley, it's white crinoline, for crying out loud! It isn't even fabric. It's supposed to go UNDER the dress," I reply sarcastically.

"I don't care, I want one. It's so sexy!"

Oh, Lord, this is going to be a long day! Could someone please tell me how I get hold of the guy who designed the *Victoria's Secret* and the *Abercrombie and Fitch* advertisements? Just give me five minutes alone with him, just five.

After the first hour we had fought over T-shirts that barely cover the bosom FROM THE BOTTOM! Jeans that cut below the pelvis and a belly button ring; and, oh yeah, "Can I get an ankle tattoo?" I'm so out of here!

A few days later when I had stopped shaking, Ashley came upstairs and said, "Mom, ya wanna see my new pink top Mike picked out for me? It's so cute! It's even girly, so you'll like it!" I glared at her, but she went and tried her "new pink girly top" on anyway.

After a full-blown runway fashion show in our kitchen, I had calmed down enough after seeing Mike's choices for them that I was back to semi-normal (if that's possible to achieve in our house just before school starts each year). "Ashley, do you know why I am opposed to you wearing the clothes you were picking?" I asked.

"Cuz you don't want me to look like a ho?" she replied.

In shock at her cut-to-the-chase answer, I agreed that it was the exact reason. I then launched into a mini-version of everything contained in this book and after about forty-five minutes, my daughters more than knew where I was coming from. The girls actually joined in with observations of their own. This was good; I had them proving my point for me.

My one daughter said that a few of the girls at school were very overweight but wore "butt-cheek" jeans and low rise shirts anyway. Then to my delight, she said, "They must have fallen for those ads, huh, Mom? They must think they make them look sexy, but they make them look silly."

I actually think I saw a glimpse of acceptance in Cassie's eyes when I was explaining that what they see in the ads and movies is not how real life or a real relationship is meant to be. Cassie is the rebel of the group, so this was a serious accomplishment for me. "The people that design these ads want you to believe that by wearing these kinds of clothes that you can make boys **love** you. They are trying to convince you that love instead of lust is what will be the end result."

"When was the last time Mike came riding up on a white horse with a rose between his teeth and swept me off my feet when I wore my Sponge Bob jammies?"

"Um, Ma! Those aren't sexy!" they laughed.

"Yeah, but the girl who was wearing them in the advertisement made them *look* that way! She gave the impression that if I wore those pants, the man of my dreams would appear out of nowhere and my new 'sexy jammie pants' would make him want and love me." I explained that advertisements often used the promised result of "love and romance" to sell a product, but that no outfit could make a person love another. They got my point.

Deflating the power of advertising in the mind of a teen is a tough thing to do when the kids around them are allowed to wear those clothes. Not all parents take the time to really consider how their kids will look in the style, and what type of image they are portraying. They either don't want to argue with their teens, don't care enough to argue, or feel guilty saying no. Guilt doesn't come from God; if you're feeling it, assume the devil is involved in the situation somewhere. Make your decision accordingly.

BOLO (Be On the Look-Out) for Written Publications

When I was younger, I used to be an avid reader of *Cosmopolitan* magazine. As time went on, I noticed the material they were publishing was being directed at a younger crowd. It seemed as if the magazine was focusing on still younger and younger women like late teens to early twenties. There was little left for a thirty-year-old mother of three to benefit from. The articles and content were becoming more and more geared towards sex and promoting sex. Not just sex with your husband, but sex with boyfriends and articles about free-spirited women who had multiple partners.

I assume that the women who bought and read this magazine were old enough to make their own decisions. But the message I was getting wasn't promoting a healthy or moral lifestyle, but instead a "party girl having a great time" type of message. It was definitely promoting a "GO OUT AND HAVE FUN WHILE YOU'RE YOUNG!" kind of attitude.

Then one day while I was waiting on my husband to get his hair cut, I noticed a *Cosmo Girl* magazine and started reading it. Same message reworded for an even younger crowd, and my daughter had been asking me to buy her this magazine. Not!!

I picked up *Seventeen* magazine thinking it would be a little less "sexy" and found the same thing. Both of these publications were promoting sexy clothes, sexy shoes, provocative hairstyles, and performers, actors, and singers who weren't sending a wholesome message of any kind.

What totally floored me after I read the article about the high school in Ohio that had the problem with teenage pregnancy was an ad on the page that followed; this ad was peddling a pubic hair template and shaving kit. For under twenty dollars I could learn how to create "fun holiday shapes." Now THAT'S what I want my sixteen-year-old daughter to have! I almost fell out of the chair.

What does she do after she's picked her shape? Does she go to school and say to her friends, "Hey, guys!!! Wanna see my palm tree?" I mean, really, what is the purpose of doing something like that unless you plan to show it off, right? Who would a teen girl show something like that to? Think about it.

Even the comics are sexually charged. I was recently exposed to a form of cartoon or comic strip called "Manga." Like Japanese *Anime*, these cartoons are drawn with out-of-proportion body parts like huge almond-shaped eyes, large breasts, tiny waists, and long legs. Another form of *Manga* is the *Pokemon* character, the little yellow guy that looks like a devil.

There is something for everyone with this particular comic style—from *Pokemon* for kids to adult *Manga* which takes on a more pornographic style with well-endowed women dressed in next to nothing. Billions of dollars are spent each year on this type of comic. Not all magazines, books, and reading materials that are supposedly for teens are FOR teens. When a magazine is titled *Seventeen*, you would assume it is for teen girls. Do you see how deceiving these things can be?

Here's how you counter it: Know what your kids are reading. Don't just assume that because the title is innocent, the publication is promoting moral content. Look at the advertisements to see what types of companies and products they are supported by. Go to the library and borrow a copy of a book they want to read or go to one of the larger bookstores that allow you to read books in their stores. Get a copy of the magazine or book your kids are interested in and peruse it before you buy it.

If you discover undesirable reading material in their possession, take it away and stand firm on the rule that they are not permitted to read it. Make it perfectly clear to them up front that certain books, magazines, etc. are forbidden and anything that is questionable needs to be reviewed by you first.

BOLO (Be On the Look-Out) for Television and Movies

I believe that there is enough information about this type of home porn invasion to fill at least a few books. It's on almost every cable channel and network. Reality shows are way too graphic for any young person to sit and watch, and some of our kids are as addicted to reality television as they are to video games.

Know exactly what your kids are watching.

Here's how you counter it: Again, know what they're watching. Before you allow them to view a program or show, take the time to view it first. Go online and look up information, ratings, reviews, and descriptions of what they're watching when you're not around. On the shows or movies that are borderline in your judgment, watch them with them so you can discuss the story, the actors and actresses, and the acting, to see which part interested them the most. Then get sneaky with a counterattack of facts about what is fantasy and what isn't.

A lot of kids aren't interested in the program for the story line, but instead have special interests in or crushes on the actors or actresses playing in these shows.

These things are the major invaders of our lives. The entire family is exposed to at least one of the above every single day. By staying alert to how the industry is trying to get into your home to accomplish their "billions of dollars" of revenue this year, you can do your part to hurt them where it counts: in their pockets! Stop buying the videos, the games, the comic books, and the magazines that keep these companies coming back to our kids for more business.

BOLO (Be On the Look-Out) for Video Games

As is the Internet, video games also are addictive. The games our teens are interested in these days are absolutely unacceptable. Have you taken the time to check out the games your kids are playing? I believe that if you did, you'd be shocked. Long gone are the days of *Pac Man, Space Invaders*, and *Centipede*. This generation doesn't even know what pinball machines are, let alone how to play them.

Aside from the fact that the average game costs $50 or more, what the actual games are promoting is horrible. I'm not talking about the sports games; I'm talking about the other stuff like *Resident Evil* (all 4 versions), *Grand Theft Auto, God of War*, and *Devil May Cry*. All of these games are rated "M" for mature. You DON'T want your kids playing them.

Grand Theft Auto–San Andreas is rated "AO" for Adults Only. Here's why. Read the game description which says:

Grand Theft Auto is back and better than ever! You ruled Liberty City, you took over Vice City, now you have a brand new city to dominate. Claw your way to the top with blazing gun battles, wild car chases, and daring crimes. Collect guns, cars, and money in this new version of a game that proves crime does pay. (Review from *shopping.com* May 8, 2006).

The last place we'd want our kids to be is in Liberty City (a section of Miami, Florida). My husband had the opportunity to work there as a policeman. Here's what he has to say about the area:

"Liberty City consists of numerous low income and subsidized housing projects harboring some of Miami Dade's toughest criminals, drug dealers, and hard core prostitutes. The atmosphere is "dog-eat-dog," and the decent residents that are stuck there are constantly living in a terrorized state. They have to worry about drive-by shootings, hypodermic needles lying on sidewalks where kids can find them, and a constant atmosphere of living in a war-zone. It unfortunately is a breeding ground for criminals and refuge for some of the worst criminals in Miami." (Michael D. Washam, Special Agent Supervisor, Retired, Florida Department of Law Enforcement [FDLE]).

This doesn't sound like a place we'd want our kids playing games. This particular series of videos has your character shooting police, high-jacking cars, and engaging in other illegal activities. There are highly graphic images with pornographic influence. Even though this game is rated for Adults Only, I only know kids who are playing it, all of whom said their parents bought it for them.

Sit and watch this video game in action and then watch the news. Do you notice the similarities? This is a real-life interactive visual that the kids with no at-home support or deprogramming can play and then go out onto the streets and think they can relive. And people say they wonder why we're seeing such a drastic increase in juvenile crime!

Here's how you counter it: There is really only one option here: DON'T BUY IT! My daughter brought home the first *Resident Evil* several years ago that she had borrowed from a friend. I was sitting next to the television on the computer when I heard all the ruckus and happened to look at what she was doing. There was a tall, sexy, well-endowed woman with a "tight leather body suit, shooting the crap out of dead people walking."

I immediately ordered her to shut the game down and return it to her friend. She then sat through a twenty-minute lecture on how that is inviting evil into her life and our home. She knew where I was coming from. A few years later she asked if she could play another game I was opposed to. I told her to go and show the game to Pastor Tom and see what he thought. She dropped the subject and it hasn't come up again. There are plenty of games that don't have sex or violence. Go online and review the games before you buy them.

BOLO MySpace.com—Breeding Grounds for Trouble

Each year the Internet brings new and exciting features. Some of the features enhance our lives and make it more convenient; others add to the list of worries we have with regard to protecting our children. Although these new services appear to be harmless and even fun, in reality they are dangerous to your kids and in some cases can be deadly.

According to *Wikipedia*, the free online encyclopedia, *MySpace* is defined as *"An American social networking Website offering an interactive, user-submitted network of friends, personal profiles, blogs, groups, photos, music and videos."*

Teens say that *MySpace.com* is the coolest hangout online. I have teens that have teen friends who all think this is the latest rave. On the surface, *My Space* appears to be pretty safe. It doesn't allow members under fourteen to create a profile, it's free and all the kids are doing it! *My Space* has security features in place like a feature that automatically restricts or privatizes the profile of anyone who is fourteen or fifteen years of age. This restriction means that the only ones who can access their personal information, which they input when signing up, are people who request to be added to their "list of friends."

Wikipedia had this to say about the child safety on MySpace—"Users whose ages are set at sixteen or over have the option to restrict their profiles and the option of allowing certain personal data to be restricted to people other than those on their friends list. Accessing the full profile of, or messaging someone when their account is set to 'private' (or if under sixteen) is restricted to a *MySpace* user's direct friends. However, this does not work as children can misrepresent their ages to bypass restrictions.

"*MySpace* often has problems with profile identity theft. These are profiles containing the pictures and sometimes information of someone else's profile. These stolen profiles are commonly used to advertise websites. *MySpace* will delete these profiles if the victim verifies their identity and points out the profile via e-mail.

"Recently, *MySpace* has been the focus of a number of news reports stating that teenagers have found ways around the restrictions set by *MySpace*, and have been the target of online predators. In response, *MySpace* has given assurances to parents that the Website *is* safe for people of all ages. Beginning in late June 2006, *MySpace* users whose ages are over eighteen could no longer be able to add users whose ages are set from fourteen to fifteen years as friends unless they already know the user's full name or e-mail address. Some third party Internet safety companies like *Social Shield* have launched online communities for parents concerned about their child's safety on *MySpace*."

Here's the problem. What if when your kids are signing up for this free, cool service they lie about their age? CLICK! Just like that their personal information is exposed for the entire world—including pedophiles, predators, and other bad guys—to see. Additionally, if they lie about their age, what else are they going to lie about? The answer to that is PLENTY!

It's not my opinion, it's fact. Listen to the news, or better yet go to your favorite search engine and look for "Articles about *MySpace*" and read them. There were too many articles for me to include in this chapter but I encourage you to search and read for yourself about the dangers of this social networking site.

Recently one of the kids in our church youth group sent me the link to his *MySpace* page. I had to go through all of the in-place security measures to be added to the list of people who could view his page. His mother monitors his *MySpace* activity very closely so he can't add just anyone without going through a process of approval. This means that not anyone can see his personal information. After I jumped all the hoops to be one of his *MySpace* friends, I began looking around his profile and clicked on his list of friends to see if I would recognize any of the kids in his list. To my complete and utter surprise, there was a picture of my daughter using a name I never would have guessed, dressed in clothes I'd never seen before. Wait, it gets worse.

Her profile was not restricted, meaning EVERYONE could see it which wasn't so bad because it was all false information, including her age which she listed as sixteen years old. The explosion from our house was probably felt around the world. When the dust had settled and we were able to sit down and talk to her, she admitted she had made the page while visiting with a church friend after school one day. Her friend confirmed this.

I monitor my kids' activity online very closely and knew there was no way she could do this from home and I knew that her school restricts access to pages like *MySpace* and *YouTube*. The only way she could have done it was from a friend's house. THANK GOD I went on to look at the other kid's page or I never would have found her page. In fact, I'm sure now that it was all God that I found it. The way she set it up was exposing her to unthinkable dangers.

I wanted to be able to list a bunch of ways to protect your kids from sites like *MySpace*, but the reality of it was brought to my attention by the same child who had violated the "No *MySpace*" rule in our house.

I asked her to tell me how someone looking for her specifically, like me or her dad, would have found her on *MySpace* and she just told it like it was.

"Mom, if you don't know the username and the e-mail address of the person you're looking for it is almost impossible to find them because you have to search through tons and tons of profiles hoping they have a picture you will recognize." Straight from the "mouth of babes."

The most effective way to protect them is to restrict them from this website. This can be done on the honor system with a warning and then trusting them to not go there. Or you can utilize a blocking program that will restrict access to any *MySpace* page including their friends' pages. You can find programs to help you accomplish this in the resource chapter at the end of the book or on my website *pornproofingyourhome.com*.

There is still the possibility that your kids are going to go behind your back and access the *MySpace*[1] website from a friend's house. This is where aggressive parenting skills come in handy. Make it a point to speak to the parents of the child your kid is visiting with about their Internet access privileges while your child is visiting. Start by letting them know that your kids are not allowed on the Internet under any circumstances. Ask them to enforce this rule with your child and be willing to do the same when their kid comes to your home. If this request is not or cannot be honored then do not allow your child to visit that home.

It is not a smart decision to allow your kid to visit with their friends when their parents aren't home. It's no different than leaving them unattended and unmonitored as was the case with my daughter and her friend. No one was there to restrict access to the material we do not allow her to access. Even though my daughter is a pretty good kid, when the temptation to go on *MySpace* was there and the peer pressure was on, she couldn't resist. Kids will still be kids.

¹ MySpace. (2007, April 9). In *Wikipedia, The Free Encyclopedia*. Retrieved 14:42, April 9, 2007, from http://en.wikipedia.org/w/index.php?title=MySpace&oldid=1213 68819.

7

Creating Safe Foundations for Your Kids

The Power and Pervasiveness of Pornography

Many of us have home insurance protection and health insurance protection. We have automobile, accident, and theft protection. We even have over-draft protection! Hardly any of us has **Porn**tection, "divine insurance" protection from the harmful and destructive effects of pornography. It is protection against a theft of family values and way of life including, but not limited to, loss of family members to explicit and addictive adult content. Overnight it seems as if the world has changed and we're all living in Pornutopia!

Too many of us have assumed that because people have the "legal right" to be immoral, the results of such a "right" is something we just have to live with. Too many of us who hate such filth simply deal with pornography by trying to avoid it. That is exactly what the enemy wants us to do, and we help him every time we allow pornography to exist without any resistance to it. Averting our attention, pretending it isn't there, has aided and abetted pornography's out-of-control growth.

The devil is quite adept at convincing the human race that pornography is simply a sign of the times and a product of so-called free speech. When I look back through the history books, I see that there have been wars over land, oil, religion, and freedom; I was hard pressed to find any documented wars over saving family values. I believe we're part of an army selected to fight the first battle of this kind.

Today our children are exposed to the message of sex almost every place they visit and on every channel they change. Even teen magazines that are meant to promote issues that interest teens, things such as hairstyles, are filled with clothes and music sprinkled with subtle pornographic messages. Men pick up a tool magazine to check out the latest socket wrenches available to the Tim Allen wannabes and they have to get past women dressed in short-shorts and cut-off shirts with big hair and even bigger chests. Not the tool kind, either! Porn is even available on our mobile phones.

Women's magazines are chock-full of sexy models wearing clothes that half the female population could never and would never wear. Teen magazines are sporting bikinis that your dad and mine would have had a heart attack over had we ever left the house in one. Even the articles are littered with pornography, a form called "erotic stories or erotic literature."

During my research I was appalled at the porn peddlers who are selling explicit images of toddlers in sexual situations today. "More babies and toddlers are appearing on the Net and the abuse is getting worse. It is more torturous and sadistic than it was before. The typical age of children is between six and twelve, but the profile is getting younger …" (Prof. Max Taylor, *Combating Paedophile Information Networks in Europe*, March 2003).

This isn't a "right" to free speech or free expression, this is criminal. Children are being sold and kidnapped into the sex trade right here in America! (February 9, 2006—ABC News Primetime—ABC News: Teen Girls' Stories of Sex Trafficking in U.S. http://abcnews.go.com/Primetime/story?id=1596778&page=1).

What amazes me even more than the fact that our babies are being exploited like this is the fact that an unbelievable number of people are actually seeking this content. The time has come to stop worrying about what people will think, or who we will offend, or who believes and who doesn't, and fall to our knees and pray for Heaven's intervention. It is our moral responsibility as Christians and our duty as parents. What would you do if it were your child being exploited; and what will you do when your child is exposed to this type of exploitation?

With the world rapidly evolving technologically, old methods of introducing this evil into families are obsolete. The dirty magazines and telephone sex of the past don't produce a fraction of the stimulation that talking to a live porn actor or actress online will create. Porn from the past just isn't as effective as it once was. The visual sensation of talking to a live model is much more powerful than looking at a still image.

To put it bluntly, we're dealing with a whole new level of invasive evil with a whole lot of power behind it. When we think of evil, we think of blood and gore; we think of an exorcist with a Linda Blair image appearing in our lives. Pornography is a different kind of evil that is being defended by our lawmakers today on the grounds of being our First Amendment "right." That's right, we have the *right* to be immoral.

Somehow, I can't imagine our forefathers sitting by the fire in good old Philly engaged in conversations about protecting pornographers' rights to freely express their pornographic material. Holy Cow! Our forefathers have to be rolling in their graves today over what has been done to their vision of our nation. If they were able, they would rise up and blast what today's elected lawmakers have made possible—all for the pursuit of the almighty dollar. Where did the godly beliefs of our early forefathers go? Who do we blame for such a decadent downslide of morality in America today?

Education is a Key to Taking Down This Industry

Before a solution to this horrible situation can be reached, we all have to understand the components that make up what experts have effectively labeled as "porn addiction." It's also necessary to understand the tactics and props the industry uses to catch your loved ones with their filth. Education is the key to taking down this industry, so understanding the tools of the industry will help us to disassemble them and loosen their grip on our families.

Pornography is a depiction of erotic behavior intended to cause sexual excitement. The unbelievable imaginations of the perversions that play into pornography is mind-boggling, outrageous, and disgusting. Add to all that the fact that pornography is addictive. Addiction is a compulsive need for and the use of a habit-forming substance or material that will alter or enhance a mood change.

If a mature, educated man can fall for the tricks the industry uses to lure him onto these sites, imagine what your kids will believe and fall victim to. The Internet is a powerful tool and it has more good features than bad. But, as with every other powerful physical, material, or earthly thing that exists in the world today, the devil has found a way to use it for evil.

I worked on the dark side of the Net, socialized with hackers, conversed with actors doing live porn chat and video while they were working, negotiated with the flesh brokers out West for content, and I have seen stuff you will fortunately never have the opportunity to see. I wish I hadn't, but if I had not seen the underbelly of this industry, you might not have had a clue about what you are really fighting against now.

I've now made it my life's mission (for the past six years) to help people pick up the pieces of their broken lives, families, and marriages. I can honestly tell you that almost half of those people found their grief online. In every single situation where I have coached a parent through a child's addiction or involvement with porn, the Internet was the culprit. Every single one of them. And in each situation, the parent could have prevented the problem but didn't take action until the damage had already been done.

Someone recently said to me that I was making it sound like there are evil monsters lurking just around the next click. There are! Just read or watch the news. How many stories have been aired about *Myspace.com* alone recently or about young girls meeting men old enough to be their grandpas because they were seduced on the Internet with lies and deceit?

Marcie's Story

One woman who contacted me was lucky enough to pick up on her daughter's nervousness before she was planning to meet some guy she thought was a boy from a neighboring school. Had she not been home sick from work that day, the results of this situation would have been tragic.

After several months, Marcie still had nightmares of what could have happened to her fourteen-year-old daughter, Abigail. So she contacted me to request prayer. After hearing about the horrible experience she went through, I asked if I could share her story. She agreed so long as I changed her family's names and location. So, here's Marcie's story:

Marcie had been feeling uneasy for over a week but couldn't put her finger on what was causing her to feel that way. Chalk it up to a mother's intuition. She noticed that her daughter, Abigail, had been spending more time online and whenever she would come into her room, Abigail would close the message she had on the screen. Marcie figured her daughter just wanted some privacy as many girls do at that age and went about her daily routines.

Normally, Marcie worked until 5:00 P.M., stopped for groceries, and headed home to arrive around 6:00 P.M. But on this Friday morning, she woke up feeling nauseous, and while she was getting dressed she became violently sick to her stomach. She called in to work and told them she was sick.

Abigail arrived home at 3:30 P.M., her normal time, and did her chores. There was no homework over the weekend, and she told her mom she was going down the road to a small park where she and her friends often met. When Marcie asked her who she was going to meet, Abigail tripped over her words and Marcie knew instinctively something was not right. Abigail wasn't the type of kid to get into trouble or to lie to her mother, so Marcie let her leave and then got dressed and went to check on her.

When Marcie pulled up to the park, she noticed an old van parked by the entrance path. For some unknown reason, she jotted down the make of the van and the tag number because "something inside told me this was not good."

She walked up the path toward the van to see a man in his late fifties holding on to her daughter's arm. The man acted as if he knew Abigail very well, but Marcie saw the look of terror and then instant relief in her daughter's eyes when she walked up. She told the man to let go of her daughter's arm, and he turned and sprinted out of the park. She noticed he was unshaven and had the look of someone who might drink a lot.

Abigail had been crying. She ran to Marcie, sobbing, and told her that the man tried to force her to go with him. She then told her mother the truth. Abigail had been blogging back and forth (online journaling) with someone she thought was a boy from a school close by. She was a cheerleader at her school, and he claimed that he was a football player from this neighboring school. After a while they started using *Yahoo Messenger* to talk in real time messages instead of posts and this "boy" convinced her that he was legit.

Her blog profile said she was a freshman at her high school, and listed her city, state, age, and physical description. There was even a picture of her in her cheerleading uniform— all totally innocent from her standpoint, but what a target for an online predator and pedophile! Little by little this man extracted further crucial data from her.

Abigail knew her mother would never agree to let her meet a boy. She knew Marcie would say that she wasn't old enough yet. But this boy had really caught her attention. She was crazy about him even though she had never seen or even talked to him on the telephone. So she agreed to sneak out and meet him. The price she almost paid doesn't even bear thinking about.

Marcie called the police and learned two days later that the van belonged to a registered sex offender who was out of prison for statutory rape. This pedophile had traveled across three counties to get to his prey and almost succeeded. Marcie has had a very hard time getting past the "what ifs," and rightfully so. Had she gone to work that day, she would not have been home in time to save her daughter.

Creating Safe Foundations

The first step toward safeguarding your family is choosing an Internet Service Provider (ISP) that offers you credible and reliable protection from the dangers of the Internet. I don't make one red cent for the recommendations I am about to make; these are just the services and software features I have used successfully for the past twelve years.

Of all of the major ISPs, *America Online* gets my vote for best online community. The features they offer me have been very successful in keeping my kids safe. My favorite feature in AOL is the *Guardian Report* and the screen name set-ups. Since I hold the master name on my AOL account, I have to set up screen names for the kids, one for each of them. When setting up the name, AOL makes sure it's really me they're talking to by asking me a secret question that only they and I know the answer to.

Once I get past that step, I type in the name I wish to create, and if it's available, it will ask me for which age category I'm creating the name. My choices are: General (full access to all features and the Web), Mature Teen (Ages 16–17), Young Teen (Ages 13–15), or Kids Only. Each age category comes with different restrictions, with the most liberal access (but not full) going to the oldest kids. Then it gets even better. I can then go into parental controls and ask AOL to restrict each one of the kids' screen names to a certain amount of time online each day (One hour in our house for the little ones, two for the oldest).

Once a day I get a Guardian Report that tells me EVERYTHING! It tells me who each kid instant-messaged, and who they sent e-mail to and received e-mail from. It tells me what sites they surfed and what parts of AOL they surfed. The best part is that I can regulate this by going into the control panel and adding or removing names, e-mail addresses, and screen names. I can restrict them from having a profile, which is the last thing you want your kid to have online!

A profile is a self-descriptive mini-Web page that contains information about the person creating it (your child). It can contain pictures and personal information and just about anything they decide to put into it. It is usually accessible to anyone (including pedophiles) who happens to search the ISP member directory.

Since I create the passwords, I can access their accounts any time I want in order to check on them. Some people might say I am invading their space. I say that as long as I am in charge of protecting their lives as my kids, I will do what I have to do to keep them from putting themselves into the dangerous reach of the predators who lurk out there waiting for kids whose parents aren't protecting them.

There are many other ISPs available to choose from, such as *PeoplePC, MSN, CharterNet* and whatever you might find in your local area, but my loyalty remains with AOL. When you choose an Internet Service Provider, make sure you choose a Filtered ISP that offers blocking and/or filtering software features. To this day, none of my children has ever received a spam mail with porn or vulgar offers in his or her mailbox.

If an ISP says it's free, expect the products and services to be worth little. When you're choosing an Internet Service Provider, don't be afraid to ask specific questions about their parental control features and what steps they take to protect young surfers from being exposed to inappropriate content. All ISPs have websites, so finding this information should be fairly easy. If you are unable to locate what you're looking for on their site, call the company. If they cannot assure you that child protection is their top priority, then don't use that service.

Internet Providers Try to Fight Back

A few years ago you only needed a good virus-protection program and maybe a software program designed to block certain sites from being accessed on your computer. The porn peddlers felt the crunch and figured out a way around these programs.

Internet Service Providers began an all-out war to compete for your family's business by adding new features for fast speeds, built-in virus protection, free music, community chat rooms, and parental controls at no extra cost. Some of these features are good, like the research resources, homework help, music downloads, and parental controls that allow you to block access to certain sites and areas. But some of their features like chat rooms and universal instant messaging are not safe for young kids or even tweens and teens.

Fast Access

It's tough to make a whopping eighteen billion dollars a year "for years to come" if your target markets can't access your websites fast enough to utilize the services you're enticing them to use. In comes fast access, and although I was quite happy to not have to pay the fees for a T1 line anymore, it opened a door to a whole new set of problems.

This fast connection feature allows people to surf the Net and download files at super fast speeds that were unthinkable only a few years ago. Remember downloading a music file on a 7400-baud connection? I used to just set it for download and go to bed and come back the next morning to get my song. Heck, it took a month to download an entire CD back then! This fast access ability to download huge amounts of information now has increased the opportunity to also fast download a lot more junk.

Fast access also made it possible to offer full-length video downloads in a fraction of the time it took to download the old *.avi* formats. Even though *.avi* formats were usually a couple of minutes in length at best, they took an hour to download. People can download videos now and watch them right on their PCs without ever leaving the house. With that new technology came the ability to download all kinds of adult videos.

This eliminated the need to sneak into the "adult" section of the local video store without being seen, and the variety online was basically endless. Anything you can imagine, whether it's legal or illegal, has all become available to anyone with a fast-access connection.

Fast access allows you to leave your computer connected to the Internet at all times, even when you aren't logged on to your ISP. For instance, I can sign off AOL, but still access the Internet through *Microsoft Internet Explorer*, a Web browser that is standard equipment on almost all computers. So, even though your kids may have used up their one-hour limit a day through parental controls that you set, they can still get online and utilize free messenger services and even set up free e-mail accounts without your knowledge.

You are comfortable thinking that they can't get online through *AOL*, or *MSN* or *PeoplePC* (or whomever your ISP is), and they have basically gone through the back door back out onto the Net—and this time *without* the protection your ISP offers! Each operating system is a little different. Again, a detailed list of instructions and resources is available on my website and updated regularly to keep up with the ever-changing technology of the Internet and computers.

You're Still the Best Protection Around

I have found that even with software safeguards in place, the best way to make sure this doesn't happen is to monitor the computer at all times or make it inaccessible without strict passwords. When everyone is offline for the day, shut the system down. Ashley is the gatekeeper in our house for the kids' computer because she has proven trustworthy. She makes everyone leave the room so they can't peek over her shoulder before she unlocks the computer for use.

Since it is impossible to stand over your kids twenty-four hours each day, you need to be sure that they aren't utilizing the freebies on the Net that allow them to communicate without the benefit of parental control restrictions. Some of these freebies are *Yahoo Messenger*, *AIM Messenger*, *MSN NetMeeting*, and others that allow a free account where you can talk real time with others who belong to their communities, even other communities. You can do this by limiting their monitored time online and utilizing one of the optional software programs I've suggested in the appendix at the end of the book.

A "community" is the environment within your ISP. For instance, paid AOL members enjoy features that people utilizing the free version (AIM) cannot access. Some of these features are chat rooms, news features, home and garden, kids' resources, and other features monitored and regulated by America Online's Terms of Service (TOS). These "paid" services are available when you sign on to your account using your user name and password. The free services are usually restricted to an e-mail account and a modified version of their Instant Messaging service. For more information about this, visit my website at www.pornproofingyourhome.com.

Kids these days are technically way smarter than most parents, and most of them know they can still surf the Web unmonitored through Internet Explorer. I have found that my best solution is Internet Blocking or Filter software that I mentioned that comes with my AOL service. Not everyone wants to use AOL and that's okay. You can purchase blocking or filter software separately.

Some other Internet safety tools (more information listed in the appendix at end of book and on my website) that will help you protect your kids are:

PC Time Monitors—These programs regulate the times of day and length of time your kids are allowed to be on the Internet.

Activity or Keystroke Loggers—These programs keep a log of all communications between your child and others so that you can later monitor what they have been doing at any time.

Pop-Up Blockers—This software will prevent unwanted ads from popping up. Pop-up ads are a major conduit for porn peddlers, and I highly recommend installing this program.

Spam Blockers—This is a program that prevents unwanted e-mail like the ones advertising porn sites, free Viagra and prescription drugs, etc., from getting through to your computer. Most filtered ISPs offer this as a standard feature.

Kid-Friendly Portals—These are sites that are safe for your kids to be on and search from. They are best used with a combination of the preventative tools above. There is a list of these portals in the appendix at the end of the book.

Porn-Alert Parents—You are the absolute best safeguard for your kids and family. No program can monitor your children like you can. There is a list of reputable software providers and a regularly updated list of resources, links, articles and tools on *pornproofingyourhome.com.*

Preventing Re-infestation from Undoing What's Been Done

In addition to what we've already addressed, there are other things you can do to make sure that the natural urges your teens are feeling don't become natural actions before they're ready.

We can't control every single thing that happens or that they are exposed to, nor do we want them to live in a vacuum. Exposure to some things is going to happen and in some cases, it will allow them to see what the real world is offering. That can also give you the opportunity to explain who, what, why, and when. Take advantage of the stuff you can't control. Here are a few suggestions. I've tried each and every one of these with successful results.

1. When a kid is talking to their crush or boyfriend/girlfriend on the phone, fifteen- to twenty-minute time limits will prevent the conversation from going into conversations that are too personal. It usually takes that long to get the small talk out of the way that leads into sexually charged subjects.

2. A cut-off time for phone use is mandatory in our home. On weekdays the cut-off is 9:00 P.M. and on weekends it's 10:00 P.M. This prevents late night calls huddled under the covers that can head down the sex path.

3. Tweenage and young teen girls (12-14) are way too young to date or be allowed out on weekend evenings with their friends without parental supervision. Don't fall for the old "Susie's mom is going with us!" VERIFY IT!

4. When older teens tell you they are going to the movies with their friends, or to the mall, or a school game, etc., pay a surprise visit to see who they're actually socializing with. This lets them know that they never know when you're going to show up unexpectedly. If you catch them doing something they know they're not supposed to do, make them leave with you and deal out the appropriate discipline.

5. Get to know their friends and their friends' parents. Make sure they have a lifestyle that is acceptable because these friends have an influence on your kid. If the kid comes from a family where there is no supervision, guidance, discipline, religious training, etc., think twice about letting your child spend a lot of time with them. Always remember to use your ripple effect praying for your kids' friends and their families, too.

6. Do a routine check of their rooms at least once a week. Look under mattresses, under beds, in the closet, in

drawers, and in boxes hidden under beds and in the closet. When you find inappropriate material, address it with them using some of the suggestions we talked about earlier.

7. Here's a fact. Teenage girls sneak out of the house! I did it, all my friends did it, and my kid's friends are doing it. When teenagers think they're in love, they'll stop at nothing to get to the objects of their affection. Drastic steps are needed here. Put alarms on windows or doors you can't monitor all the time like upstairs or doors away from your range of hearing. Home improvement stores sell a battery-operated version at a more affordable price than an alarm company. Don't let your kids know they are there.

A friend of mine has a baby monitor downstairs so she can hear when the door that her kid will most likely try to sneak out of is opened. She has caught her daughter trying to sneak out on two occasions. Her daughter assumed she was up and heard her, and doesn't know the monitor is there.

8. Restrict cable or satellite access to channels that you know air inappropriate shows or movies. Don't let them use guilt to persuade you to change this.

9. Choose an Internet Service Provider that offers parental control and reporting features like *AOL's Guardian Report*. (See the chapter on Porn Peddlers and Spammers and Pedophiles for more resources).

10. Always confirm with parents when a sleepover is involved and be sure the parents are responsible people. If it's possible, suggest the kids sleep over at your house. My girls aren't allowed to spend the night away from home unless it is with someone from church; we have a routine where we call to let each other know the kids are in for the night, etc. Set up a buddy system with other parents you do trust to let your kids stay with.

As a parent who has made so many of the mistakes your kids are trying to make, you know what's right and what isn't. When you're feeling unsure or guilty, take it to the Lord in prayer. He'll guide you in peace down the path you need to go.

Always have names of their friends' parents, addresses, and phone numbers on hand and USE THEM! Don't be afraid of embarrassing your kids by calling and asking to speak with them while they are away.

8

Dealing with Filth Slithering into Your Home

Get Rid of Cyber Space Trips to Faraway Places

Would you let your child travel alone around the world to exotic places like Amsterdam, Brazil, Singapore, or even closer to home—Las Vegas, New York, or the red light district of Miami? Me neither! Just because you may consider they are safe at home behind their monitor and keyboard doesn't mean they are.

Just like traveling around the world to every country, the Internet allows us to do the same from the comfort of our homes. The problem is that our families face the same dangers and temptations as if they were physically traveling to these places.

If your husband were to travel on business to Bangkok, the chances are that he would come into contact with at least one woman who would offer to make all of his fantasies come true for a price. It's the nature of the beast in places like that and many men go there just for that reason. Your husband, being the good man that he is, would of course be tempted. Hopefully he'd have the power to refuse and would return home to you just as pure as when he left.

On the Internet, he could be visiting a sports website when a "pop-up" pops up and confronts and tempts him. He really wouldn't be physically cheating on you if he just peeked; he'd only be looking, right? No, he couldn't do that, he thinks, because folks at church would never understand if they found out. But that same temptation keeps popping up in front of him, day after day, night after night. Every time he signs online, the temptation is there.

The women are just so beautiful and they don't have any clothes on; it's just too much to resist. He buys off on the free trial and the women who enticed him to enter in the first place are nowhere to be found, but there is an equally attractive girl waiting for him in the live video chat. Her job is to seduce and she is good at it. She makes some casual chitchat and finds out what his deepest desires are. That's all it takes for him to keep going back "just one more time." He really isn't physically cheating, after all; he's just curious.

This isn't a made-up scenario; this is how one clergyman became addicted to pornography. He said, "My wife is a good conservative Christian woman; she never would have understood or even considered indulging in the perverted fantasies I was able to live out in my mind in these video chat rooms." The woman he continued to visit online was as good at sales as she was at keeping her customers happy. The cost for this service at the time was $2.99 per minute. "She had no scruples at all. She did anything I told her to do and even offered to meet me for a rather large sum of money. I'm telling you, if I'd had the money, I would have gone."

Once the devil hooks into a man's thoughts, it becomes the battle of his life. Adding to that problem is the fact that he's at a point where he's not really sure he wants to win the battle. The key is to not let the enemy into your thoughts or into any area of your life to begin with!

Knowing the Enemy—The Components of Porn

These days porn comes wrapped in many alluring, colorful packages. Here are some of the main gift boxes of pornography that will be put forth to try to entice your loved ones:

• **Magazines and Print Formats** such as *Hustler*, *Playboy*, centerfolds, etc. These forms of pornography are available in adult bookstores and even in many convenience stores. They are the magazines located behind the counter with a blocker placed in front of them which allows just enough of the magazine's front cover to be exposed to tempt the buyer into wanting more. Amazing what digital photography can do.

• **Strip Clubs and Live Adult Entertainment Establishments** are organizations which provide the visitor (almost always men) with an ability to interact in person with women who strip and perform limited intimate acts for a price. Alcohol flows freely and the more the guys drink, the more they spend on "special services" such as lap dances and private shows. These strip joints often employ women who also illegally engage in the act of prostitution. These gals are motivated by money to make each man feel like they are the greatest thing since sliced bread; as a result, the guys keep going back.

• **Phone Sex and Adult Conversation Lines** with women who sound incredibly attractive and will tell the callers anything they want to hear. These calls include simulating the act of live sex over the phone line. Unfortunately, the pictures they use to advertise these sex lines are usually of beautiful young women when in reality the man is most likely speaking to a world-weary, bleary-eyed, haggard woman eating pizza and bonbons on the other end of the line.

• **Adult Online Chat Lines** that come complete with file-sharing to exchange pictures providing voice as well as text-chat capabilities. Many men and women meet on these chat lines for risqué chat.

• **Adult Classifieds** in which men and women create profiles which are NEVER the complete truth. Some examples are: "Single male, 20 years old, 6 feet-3 inchs tall, 175 pounds, six-figure income, likes to workout, sail my yacht on weekends, and dine out on caviar is looking is for 18-

year old female who wants to spend the rest of her life playing in the sun."

In reality, you're more than likely speaking to a fifty-four-year-old balding man with bad breath, a beer belly, and a job as a can opener for the local bean factory who is married to his third wife and has eight kids. You can be anyone you want to be when you're hiding behind a printed ad. I have known many men and women who were absolutely nothing like the descriptions they placed in these personal ads. The more enticing the personal description, the better the visual the users can create in their minds.

• **Adult Content Websites** offer streaming video and the capability to play movies on the viewers' computers. These adult content websites have exploded across the Internet in staggering numbers. After paying a small fee which is billed to the visitor's credit card under a fictitious name like "AnyCompany, Inc.," the user can discreetly download pornographic images, videos, profiles, and more. Most of these sites offer the added value (for another charge!) of live adult shows with actors performing live on the screen.

• Many sites now offer interactive features which allow the visitor or member the option of engaging in one-on-one conversation with the model or actor. These personalized services usually cost extra and the better the actress on the other end, the more money the visitor will spend in a "private" chat with her.

These gals are well trained in how to retain their audience. They make the men who visit feel like they are gods, telling them things that boost their ego while showing them things that tempt them into coming back for more. Many of these actresses do "command performances," with the man telling her what to do.

Man after man, night after night, session after session— these girls tell the men who visit each day exactly what they think they want to hear. They make the men feel like they are the only ones in life who matter. To a guy who has fallen into what he thinks is a mundane marriage and a boring job, these girls make him feel alive again. He ignores the fact that when his time is up, she'll be "entertaining" someone new.

Very often the video quality is grainy and the lighting is poor which makes it difficult for the man who visits to see what he's really getting for his money. Young, old, black, white, fat, skinny, teens who are not really teens but made up to look that way, homosexuals, people with fetishes, you name it—the Internet porn industry has them all. And they know how to accommodate every addiction.

• **Adult-Oriented Newsgroups** are the gateway to uncensored worldwide porn. From the brothels in Vegas to the red-light districts in Singapore and Amsterdam, you can find almost anything on a newsgroup including illegal content. In the United States it is illegal for minors to perform in the industry and for porn site owners to use minors. Legitimate companies verify the age of their models or actresses before they are allowed to perform.

Not all countries obey those laws, nor do many private parties. Newsgroups have been known to have true "kiddie porn" and other illegal content such as bestiality, etc.

But Aren't These Just Unemployed, Unattractive, Tired-Out Losers who Use These Services?

USA Today, March 23rd, 2006, featured an article by Jayne O'Donnell called "Should Execs Conduct Business at Strip Clubs?" which revealed that many business executives take their male clients to upscale strip clubs to conduct business. Some of these businessmen are paying four hundred dollars or more for a lap dance or time spent in a private room (an additional $200 per hour) with a stripper.

The girls are making thousands of dollars per day, the men are living their fantasies, and their wives are at home raising the kids and keeping house. This is not the way God intended it to be.

These are just some of the most common forms of pornography. The porn industry has created fantasy situations just right to hook anyone who is even slightly tempted or curious to delve deeper into the dark side of the porn industry. Once these pornographers have hooked their prey, it's a true battle to set them free.

This is not an easy war we're fighting; but it is a war that has invaded your home and your family, and the only way you're going to win is to fight back. The key to winning this war is being properly equipped physically, spiritually, emotionally, and mentally. The battle for your loved one can be emotionally draining and can ultimately start to affect your mental health if you're not equipped to deal with it.

What are some of the others forms of evil slithering into your home?

Adware Innocent? NOT!

One of the worst inventions ever to hit the Internet is the pop-up advertisement which is the most commonly used advertisement for porn sites. The second worst invention is adware. Together, these two elements can make the Internet a most frustrating and even obscene experience. Add an unmonitored fast access or DSL connection to the equation and you're opening the door for the porn peddlers that no ISP can prevent.

According to *Webopedia*, the Internet's number one online encyclopedia dedicated to Internet technology, adware is considered a legitimate alternative offered to consumers who do not wish to pay for software. Programs, games, and utilities can be designed and distributed as freeware. Sometimes freeware blocks features and functions of the software until you pay to register it.

Today we have a growing number of software developers who offer their goods as "sponsored" freeware until you pay to register. Generally most or all features of the freeware are enabled but you will be viewing sponsored advertisements while the software is being used. The advertisements usually run in a small section of the software interface or as a pop-up ad box on your desktop. When you stop running the software, the ads should disappear. This allows consumers to try the software before they buy and you always have the option of disabling the ads by purchasing a registration key.

In many cases, adware is a legitimate revenue source for companies who offer their software free to users. A perfect example of this would be the popular e-mail program, *Eudora*. You can choose to purchase *Eudora* or run the software in sponsored mode. In sponsored mode, *Eudora* will display an ad window in the program and up to three sponsored toolbar links. *Eudora* adware is not malicious, and it reportedly doesn't track your habits or provide information about you to a third party.

This type of adware is simply serving up random paid ads within the program. When you quit the program, the ads are supposed to stop running on your system. Unfortunately, some freeware applications which contain adware do track your surfing habits in order to bombard you with other ads specifically related to your interests. When the adware becomes intrusive like this, then it moves into the spyware category and becomes something you should avoid for privacy and security reasons.

Due to its invasive nature, spyware has really given adware a bad name. Since any form of adware, malicious or not, is an annoyance, I have yet to meet anyone who actually likes it or benefits from it. I strongly urge you to do whatever you have to do to avoid all forms of it. (Modified from content in Webopedia.com by writer Vangie Aurora Beal, 11/11/04, original content used by permission).

You can teach your kids to avoid this stuff by forbidding them to download anything that says it's free. This includes screensavers, software, and games that say they are free. If you stick with the "you get what you pay for" philosophy, it will be pretty easy for you to identify these conduits.

Spyware—It's Free, Nekkid, and You'll Be a Millionaire!

Webopedia tells us that spyware is considered to be a malicious program which is similar to a *Trojan Horse*. Users unwittingly end up installing the malicious program when they install something else. A common way to become a victim of spyware is to download certain peer-to-peer file-swapping products that are available today.

Once installed, the spyware monitors your computer user activity on the Internet and transmits that information in the background to someone else. Truly invasive spyware can gather information from your computer files about your e-mail addresses, passwords, and credit card numbers. Spyware exists as independently executable programs with the capability to monitor your keystrokes, scan files on your hard drive, and snoop into other applications such as chat programs or word processors. Spyware can install other spyware programs, read cookies on your computer, and change your default home page on the Web browser.

Again, spyware does this while consistently relaying the information back to the spyware author who will either use it for advertising and marketing purposes, or sell the information to another party which could involve theft of your identity.

Licensing agreements that accompany software downloads sometimes warn the user that a spyware program will be installed along with the requested software, but the licensing agreements are rarely read completely by users. This notice of the spyware installation is often couched in obtuse, hard-to-read legal disclaimers (Webopedia.com, writer Vangie Aurora Beal, 11/11/04, used by Permission).

This is sneaky stuff, isn't it?

With all of these new computer-penetrating invaders like spyware, adware, PC snoopers, and Phishing programs, then we have the spammers who have been annoying us with their Viagra ads for years. Is there really ANYBODY who actually answers these Viagra ads? As spam prevention and regulation of the Internet has increased, these dirtballs have resorted to utilizing free messenger services that nearly all ISPs offer so they can bombard you with their porn messages. You can be surfing a recipe website when all of a sudden an Instant Message pops up and says: *"Hi, I'm Jody, 23/F blonde, blue eyes, 5 feet-6inches, 122 pounds. Come see my free nekkid pictures on www.seeJodynekkid.com."*

I utilize my "REPORT SPAM" button plenty and personally with these. Your ISP most likely offers an "anti-spam" feature. Check the FAQ's (Frequently Asked Questions) to learn more about how to utilize this feature on your e-mail service. I am also on to all these millionaires in Africa who just happened to pick little old me out of seventy million Internet users so they can wire twelve million dollars into my bank account. How nice of them.

Isn't it just too generous of them to offer me half of that money for letting them use my bank account to launder the money they have inherited from their dead fathers, uncles, or brothers who just happened to be the ambassadors to some unknown country? Right!

Now imagine yourself as a sixteen-year-old boy surfing the Net with raging hormones when Jody comes offering her free peek. Never mind that he's talking to a robot software program designed to message anyone who is shown as actively online in the member directory of his ISP. Never mind that it is probably some other kid on the other end getting paid by the click to spend his entire life sending these messages out.

This reminds me of an article on *MSNBC.com* I recently read about a thirty-year-old North Carolina man, Mr. Jaynes, who was considered among the top ten spammers in the world at the time of his arrest. He used the Internet to peddle pornography, and sham products and services such as being a "FedEx refund processor," prosecutors said. Thousands of people fell for his e-mails, and prosecutors said Jaynes' operation grossed up to $750,000 per month.

That's a lot of money! (© *The Associated Press*—May 8, 2006 MSNBC.com)

Another Buffalo, New York, man was sentenced three-and-a-half to seven years for sending out over 800 million e-mails through the Earthlink network. EIGHT HUNDRED MILLION! WOW! (Paul Roberts, *IDG News Service—PCWorld.com*—May 8, 2006).

The companies that pay these people for every click they harvest don't monitor who or how their "employees" are getting their message out. They only care that it's getting out. The tracking programs installed on the ads tell them how many people have actually clicked the ad. The person who sends them out is paid for every click, usually some ridiculously low amount like five cents, by a marketing company that is paid to advertise the business, product, or service being displayed in the pop-up ad.

To earn $20,000, you'd have to send millions of ads. Since we know that the largest group of viewers of Internet porn is teen boys ages twelve to seventeen, it's safe to say that these ads are targeting our sons in staggering numbers.

If you've been the victim of adware on your computer, then you know the ridiculous number of pop-up ads that you may have had to get through just to open a non-Internet based program. And that's before you even sign onto your ISP!! With fast access, these adware programs run even when you are not using your ISP. Now multiply that by seventy million computers or at the very least fifty million. That's a lot of exposure.

All your innocent and naïve son knows is that it said FREE, it's NEKKID, and all he has to do is click on it. Two points for the porn peddler who is getting paid to produce clicks. He got another statistic and made another nickel, and your kid can't wait to get online again to get the next message! He starts living for those random messages that he thinks are from some girl who randomly picked him out on the entire World Wide Web.

And The Beat Goes On

During one hour when I recently monitored my messages while writing, I received four Instant Messages from non-AOL members, meaning the people who are messaging me aren't members of my AOL community, but they are using AOL's Free Messaging service.

From January to April 2006, I was receiving these messages from senders with screen names like **Ghu76543333**. Common sense tells me that no legitimate person would choose that as a screen name. It's generated by a software program designed to randomly pick names in numerical sequence. They have to do this because as folks report these messages to AOL as spam, AOL blocks the name and they have to create a new one to start messaging again.

I clicked on these first messages and they immediately went into the "Hi, I'm Jody..." routine. To avoid detection as a spammer, the person initiating these messages didn't type in the Web address as www.jodyisnekkid.com because as soon as they hit enter, it would become a hot link and my filter would kick it back. Instead, they typed the Web address in as www(dot)nameofsite(dot)com and give me instructions to replace the (dot) with a (.). They are soooo slick.

Lately these porn peddlers have been sending me messages that start with "Hey!" as if they are trying to strike up a conversation with me. Not knowing who one such person was, I clicked on respond and typed back, "Do I know you?" I instantly received the porn link in response. I consider myself pretty Internet savvy but if I fell for it, surely a young person will. In order for the sender to get their actual link in front of potential buyers, they have to get a response to their message first.

If you don't know who is sending you a message, don't answer it! I can't stress the importance of this precaution enough because it is one of the most common avenues that the bad guys use to coax personal information from your unknowing child. If your ISP offers the feature, go into parental controls and click the option that allows you to block ALL Internet messages from getting through.

Another Day, Another Door, and They're In Again

When one thing doesn't work, the bad guys immediately start trying another. So, I wish I could tell you that a one-time blocking, fixing, rejecting, or whatever you do would protect anyone using your computer. It won't. You have to keep up with the monitoring and protecting of your computer every day, or don't let anyone use it unless you're sitting right there with them.

While you may not realize it, the bad guys may have already managed to install spyware on your computer. There are some signs that tell you that the spyware is there. If you notice any changes to your Web browser that you did not make such as extra toolbars or different homepage settings or changes to your security settings and favorites list, you could have spyware running on your system.

Other signs of a spyware infection include tons of pop-up ads which aren't related to a website you're viewing. Spyware advertisements are usually adult content in nature and are not displayed in the same fashion as legitimate ads you would normally see on your favorite websites. You may also see advertisements when you're not browsing the Web. Clicking hyperlinks which do not work (or that take you somewhere you didn't expect), a sluggish system, or your system taking longer to load the Windows desktop are all signs that your computer may be infected with spyware.

With the onset of spyware has come a plethora of anti-spyware software packages to rid your system of these unwanted and malicious programs. Anti-spyware software works by identifying any spyware installed on your system and removing it. Since spyware installs itself like any other application installed on your system, it will leave traces of itself in the system registry and other places on your computer. Anti-spyware software will look for evidence of these files and delete them if found.

Much like a firewall or anti-virus program, anti-spyware software is crucial to maintain optimal protection and security on your computer and network. (Modified from content in Webopedia.com, Writer Vangie Aurora Beal, 11/11/04, used with permission).

Of course, the best approach to adware and spyware is to avoid it. Without knowing it, my son had downloaded over 1,700 spyware and adware modules on our computer two years ago. He thought he was getting free Sponge Bob screen savers and games, but in reality he was simply giving the porn peddlers their way into our home.

The technology changes almost daily and as the protective measures catch up with the predators, they find another way to invade. Staying current on these issues is a must in order to keep your family safe. Be sure to update your software regularly and visit *pornproofingyourhome.com* for the latest information available.

9

Modern Day Deborahs: Solo Moms and Single-Minded Warriors

Accepting and Dealing with the Way Things Are Now

There were many times during my years as a single mom when I felt totally hopeless and overwhelmed at the things I had to protect my kids from and teach them about. But after seeing how many kids were falling by the wayside by getting into drugs, teenage pregnancies, criminal issues, and just plain mischief, I realized that the issues these kids were being lost to could have been prevented.

I am not talking about these issues being prevented by the schools, by the government, or even the Church. These are issues that should have been prevented by these children's parents stepping up to the plate and taking responsibility for protecting their children. I decided that somehow I would find a way to do this for my kids.

Some of the women I deal with are angry with God for their circumstances. They feel they've received the short end of the bargain in life and they are myopically focused on how unfair it is that they are left with the responsibility of raising kids while their ex-spouse seems to be living his life carefree. I tell them that you can't blame God for choices you made. His perfect will for their lives never included sending them the wrong partners; they chose them!

Since you can't go back and change what was done, you only have the option of moving forward and making things better. So, now is as good a time as any to realize that if your ex isn't in the picture or doesn't support the path you are trying to take to protect your kids from the dangers of this world, you are going to have to go it alone at least for the time being.

If you're a single parent and your kids come first and foremost before anything else, then good for you! You're a rarity these days. Just like Deborah in the biblical Book of Judges, Chapter Four, it may seem to you as if the men have all faded into the woodwork or "left the building." They came around for a while, played a little house, and then decided it wasn't for them. Then they ran away and left the women to be the leaders of their families.

The single mothers these runaway men leave behind find themselves in a position of having to be both Mom and Dad to sons and daughters while trying to figure out a way to support their families. It's a miracle any time single mothers do a good job at both of these priorities and still find a way to keep their own heads balanced and focused in a positive manner. To anyone who has never been a single mom, this probably sounds impossible. But for those of us who have done it and are doing it, it's just a way of life.

As we were finishing up the editing portion of this book, my editor Liberty Savard sent me the one message I had managed to escape up to this point in the book-editing process.

"Houston, we have a problem!" the subject line read. I almost dreaded opening the e-mail, but what we thought would be a problem was actually an *opportunity* for me to take this special section for single moms further, to take it right on to where God wanted me to take it. He knows that single moms need special attention, and I feel the need to elaborate on a few things for you. I thought we might look at some of the opportunities you have to be a true Modern Day Deborah!

Opportunities, Not Problems

Not too long ago we had a crisis in our family and my mom said to me "This is not a problem, it's an opportunity." I now try to apply that to all the issues that arise in my life that attempt to cause me "problems."

Being a single parent with all of its challenges can appear to be riddled with problems at times. But these challenges offer the perfect opportunities for you to shape a life, guide a vulnerable and naïve young mind, and produce a well-balanced, productive, and wonderful human being—your child. As you do this, you can thank the Lord for helping you to earn a well-deserved pat on your back!

The Opportunity to Pray

I am a firm believer in the power of prayer in all situations. I believe the power of prayer is needed even more in single mom situations for strength, guidance, and for miracles for every area of your life. Okay, let's make a list:

- Do you worry about how the bills are going to get paid?
- Do you worry about what the kids are doing when you're not home because you have to work?
- Do you worry about what they might be getting into or who they are hanging out with while you're working to support them?
- Are you working and going to school to try to better yourself and their life?
- Do you feel like you're never going to have a life of your own?
- Do you believe God intended for your life to be this way?

I don't believe God has wanted you stressing out about a single one of these things. Not for a second. The Lord is the answer and has an answer for everything you are dealing with. Although He has inspired me to share some ways to cooperate with His solutions for your situation, He is still your first resort.

God's Word says, *"You have not because you ask not..."* (James 4:2). Have you ever thought about what you really want from the Lord with respect to being a single parent? Here's an example of how to pray to begin getting into alignment with His will and His perfect future for you and your children:

Heavenly Father, I am so thankful for the gift of children You have blessed me with and for the strength and ability and grace You are more than willing to pour out upon me to help me raise them. Lord, I know You can see what the world is doing to our kids today, and I know that this isn't what You want for me and mine. Father, I come before You asking forgiveness for not believing that You will make a way for me to be the mother You intended me to be to my children. I have tried to make this work by myself, but I am ready to surrender this situation to You so that I may do this in harmony with Your perfect will. Please Lord, make a way for me to be here to protect and guide them and to also support and provide for them as well. Help me believe that this is possible because right now it looks totally impossible. Guide my steps and open doors to opportunities that I can step through that will allow me to be a single mom testimony to Your love and grace and miracles. Help me to be an example so other single moms will realize they can turn to You, too. In Jesus' name, I pray this, believing You will make a way for me to make a way. Amen.

Opportunities to Believe

Being a single mom can be very tough work with little inspiration and hope at times. It might even appear completely hopeless at times, but I am going to tell you right now that God wants you to change your thinking because He has something so much better for you.

God wants to place people and even tools like this book in front of you to guide you toward the wonderful miracles He has for you. He has miracles with your name on them that will make being a single mom not only easier with the blessed results, but they will also be part of your testimony to other single moms. You can have a testimony about what He's done for you to even show those who might not believe in God's great goodness that there is a better way to protect your kids and still provide for them.

Praying the above prayer and *all* the other prayers in this book will lift your head, lighten your heart, and give you faith to know that with God ANYTHING is possible! That's not my opinion; it's God's promise! In Matthew 19:26, Jesus said, *"With man this is impossible, but with God all things are possible"* (NIV).

Are you wondering how to manifest these miracles in your single mom situation? Well, of course the answer is FAITH in God's love and personal concern for you and your children! The prophet Jeremiah was asked by God, *"Is anything too hard for me?"* (Jeremiah 32:27). The answer to that is NO!

I know it's easier said than done to "simply believe," but here is where you need to start right now. Determine in your mind that God will answer; then declare to your soul that you are asking God to give you the faith you need to pray this miracle to life. When your faith wavers, ask Him again to help you believe! When the kids start acting out or answering back, call down the power of heaven (through prayer) and *believe* that God is right next to you parenting those kids alongside you. Let Him guide and direct you. As you pray, believe that God is hearing your request for help and guidance, and then be still and listen for His voice of guidance in your heart.

Embrace the fact that what you are doing would have been unthinkable a few decades ago. You are raising kids in a sex-saturated, violent, drug-infested world and you and

God are going to raise them right! This may not be easy, but it is doable and it is flat-out admirable.

You don't need to plan ahead or schedule this new way of thinking for some time in the future; you can make up your mind to start this way right this very second. This is your *opportunity* to believe and expect that God will make a way. He will make the way and all you need to do right now is *simply believe* that He will. He will let you know what you need to do to cooperate with Him as He does.

Opportunity to Set New Boundaries

Earlier, I pointed out that God sometimes makes us wait for answers. When He does this, He's training us and preparing us for the miracle to come. In a single-mom situation, this is really no different. Sometimes we have to learn new skills first in order to nurture and protect the miracle in the making, that being to raise children who are products of a God-influenced home. Remember, it all starts at home.

One of the most common things we fail to do in single-mom situations is to set firm boundaries with our kids. We're usually too tired to argue with them, so we let them get away with some things that can be dangerous, such as phone time after a respectable hour, staying out later than it's safe to do, and having unmonitored time online. I know it's easier to just let them do it because you don't have to find the energy to fight with them. But you're going to get out of this what you put into it. Starting **today**, set some new boundaries.

Phone Time—Nothing good comes from unlimited time on the telephone, especially when they're talking to the opposite sex. Limit their calls and their time on each call. Set time limits for phone use; i.e., no calls at all after 10:00 P.M. on school nights, and 11:00 P.M. on weekends. Explain that phone use is a privilege, and when it's violated, be sure to stick to the penalties. Usually taking phone time away for a night or more (depending on the infraction) cures this pretty quickly.

My daughter is a social butterfly and last year she received so many phone calls from so many different kids that it seemed as if our phone never stopped ringing. After catching her on the phone one evening very late talking to an older boy, we took her phone privileges away for one week. When we reinstated her privileges, she was only allowed three calls a night of twenty minutes each. When she was caught violating the rules again, she lost more time. It didn't take long for her to realize that I meant business, and we haven't had a problem in almost a year.

Making rules and sticking to them works.

You get out of this what you put into it. Set the rules and then enforce them!

Curfew—Having lived in big cities and in small towns I learned that after a certain time, usually 10:00 or 11:00 P.M., there is absolutely NOTHING for kids to do except get into trouble. There are few exceptions to this, if any. If you're the type of single parent who is comfortable with your teen or tween being out after that, then you are part of the problem and you're asking for more trouble than you'll be able to handle.

This isn't a matter of IF trouble will happen, it's a matter of WHEN trouble will happen. Set boundaries and a curfew that is safe for your child even if he insists he'll be the dork of the crowd for having to be in so early. Better that he be a dork than find him dead or worse.

Get your kids in the house by 11:00 P.M. or earlier and stick to that rule! If they fight it, tell them they can't go out at all and then stick to that, too. There is no worse restriction for a teen than keeping them in when their friends are out. It's pure torture to hear them describe it. Knowing that you're going to stick to your promise to keep them in, they'll learn not to cross the line.

Remember, YOU'RE THE PARENT. Explain that you're protecting them and leave it at that. It shouldn't be open for discussion!

Internet—This is as serious as staying out late. Single-mom situations usually involve a mom who is exhausted after working all day or perhaps working and going to school. If you were like I was, you fall face first into bed by 10:00 P.M. Do your kids have Internet access after you're in bed? Do you know where they're surfing or who they're talking to? Do you ever get up and check on them? Do you have special software than can show you their online activity?

Just because they're in the house in the room next to you doesn't mean they're safe. Set a time for online activity. For instance, tell them that after 10:00 P.M. there is no more surfing. This works very well in my home. Check out some of the resources I have provided for ways and software that will ensure they won't go back online after you're in bed and then **utilize them!** If you catch them breaking the rules, take away their Internet privileges. In some cases, if they are caught breaking the time rule or they are surfing a restricted site, combine the privileges you restrict like no phone or Internet for two days.

These are just a few of the most common issues single moms tend to go light on. They are also the most dangerous. Additionally, these are the privileges that children of single moms tend to take the most advantage of because they know Mom is too tired, too busy, or too preoccupied to really enforce them.

The key to success is consistency. Set the rules and stick to your guns.

Manners and Respect

Single moms are usually so caught up in providing for and raising their kids with what little energy they have left that they often leave out the important stuff like simple manners and respect for others, especially teachers. Have you taught your children to hold their tongue when a teacher or elder is speaking to them, even if they don't agree with what is being said? I have witnessed more and more kids who argue and even get nasty in some situations. Do you allow this sort of behavior at home?

How can you expect your kids to have simple manners like respecting others if they are allowed to be disrespectful to you? How about table manners, or simple things like saying please, thank you, or holding a door open for the person coming in behind them? I almost NEVER see these kinds of manners in the kids I encounter today. These are basic manners that show class.

If this is something you haven't paid much attention to, you might want to do a Manners Inventory and quiz your kids about their basic manner skills. If you see they are lacking in this area, now is as good a time as any to start teaching them what they need to know about being respectful and mannerly. Perhaps work on one manner at a time, explaining the value and the benefits of this particular manner.

A lot of single moms have little or no time to teach their kids about God, and we need only look around to see how this is affecting our single-mom families and society as a whole. Remove God, remove goodness.

The Reward System

Every day has new *opportunities* for single moms. Teens and tweens and even younger kids can be taught that it is to their advantage to not answer back, to do their chores with a good attitude, to be prompt at finishing up school work, and many other such things. Make sure they understand expectations, boundaries, penalties, and beneficial possibilities (in addition to the rewards you may give them). Once you have these in place, you can develop a reward system.

Young kids, teens, and tweens respond very well to the reward system. Whether it is an extra privilege or a material reward, it gives them the incentive to keep doing a good job. A reward can turn a possible reaction into a positive action. Let the rewards fit the accomplishment, and be sure to make good on them. This is a tried and proven system for success for single moms.

Single Moms Searching for a Soul Mate

"They're lonely, tired, and they feel like they've been cheated out of a good life that everyone else seems to have …" This is what Liberty Savard (my editor and a fellow former single mom) said when we discussed this chapter. She hit the nail on the head. This is not just a single mom dilemma, though; it's more of a woman thing. I know quite a few married women who feel the same way, too. Now that I think about it, I know some men who feel this way as well!

Without a doubt, the most common issue single moms deal with is loneliness and a belief that finding a "significant other" could make everything better. This component of a single mom's life can be the "maker" or the "breaker" of so many single-mom situations with regard to the mental and emotional well-being of their children.

My ministry deals with more women who are willing to sacrifice the well-being of their children for men they think they "love" than I can write about in ten books. I don't need to research statistics on this topic because my ministry (*just4ladies.com*) gets a whopping 3.2 million visitors every month with over sixty percent of them being single moms who are in "love" situations that are causing them to neglect their children and themselves. I create my own statistics from this website.

Let's start at the root of this situation and identify a healthy "love" relationship for a single mom or any woman for that matter. There are a few components that make up true love, and without them, the "love" you think you're feeling is a sham.

Respect

The most important component is respect. If the person you are so "in love" with doesn't respect you and you accept that, it's time for you to take a closer look at who you're sharing your most precious possession (your heart) with.

Have you ever heard the saying, "Do as I say, not as I do?" This might sound good, but the children of a single mom are going to do as she does. What she does will far too often outweigh and override what she says.

If you're raising little girls, you are teaching them that it is acceptable to be with someone who doesn't respect you. You are teaching them that it is all right to accept being treated with no respect just so that you are not alone. If you tend to date multiple men who treat you with no respect, you're further instilling this destructive and unhealthy behavior in your little girl's head. She will go on to choose the same kind of man who treats her with little or no respect and never recognize the destructiveness of this pattern of thinking because she only has you as a role model to go by.

For the little men you are raising, you are exposing them to male figures who are disrespectful and still get what they want, perhaps even more. A little boy is going to pick up on those traits because these are the male figures you're exposing him to. My guess is that he will begin or already has begun showing you a lack of respect as his mother because he sees you tolerate it out of the men you choose to be with.

Men like this do nothing to contribute to the well-being of your children. They don't sit down with them and teach your sons the right way to treat a woman. They don't sit down with your daughters and teach them how to avoid boys who are only after "one thing." Guys like this have no respect for themselves or for you, so how can you expect them to teach your precious children this most important value? You can't.

Ask yourself why you've chosen to be with someone who doesn't respect you. The most common answer I hear is, "So I'm not alone." That's not good enough, Girlfriend! You are WAY too precious in God's eyes to accept that and your kids are too!

Trust

The second most important component of a "true love" relationship is trust. There is nothing worse in a relationship than lack of trust. Choosing a cheater to "love" is an emotionally draining lifestyle. It violates the "respect" component in every form. A cheater and a liar will take so much time and energy away from your life and the lives of your kids that it will leave little for anyone involved, including yourself.

Choosing to love a man you can't trust sets an unhealthy example for your kids. Choosing a cheater means that you often spend time and energy trying to find out who he's with, what he's doing, and where he is. In addition to that, you're hurting over the things he keeps doing to violate your trust. This means little emotional support left over for your children.

As they learn that your attention is so focused on finding out where your man is and what he's doing, they learn that they can get away with a multitude of things like staying out late, seeing wrong friends, and getting into mischief like drugs or drinking. Shame on the single mother who is too focused on her missing man to even notice that her kid is coming home at 2:00 A.M. half-tanked or higher than a kite.

This child will also start to wonder why you don't love them enough to expend that same kind of energy caring about them. They may purposely act out to get your attention off this man and on to themselves, even if it means they have to get into trouble to do it.

Loving an Unbeliever

Okay, you've asked God into your life and you're now determined to pray BIG miracles into your single-mom situation. The problem is, however, your boyfriend is not a believer. Maybe he even makes fun of your faith. The Bible says this: *"Do not be yoked together with unbelievers. For what do righteousness and wickedness have in common? Or what fellowship can light have with darkness?"* (2 Corinthians 6:14, NIV).

I often hear single moms complain that their "significant other" is not a Christian, but they are believing that they can change him. I've even had some girls tell me that this particular verse of Scripture doesn't apply in today's world because there are so many unbelievers. Let me tell you something, God is the same yesterday, today, and tomorrow.

Jesus Christ didn't pay the price for your sins and to give you a brand new chance at life so you could make your own rules, overriding what God knows is best for you! Giving the Lord half your heart and half a commitment is setting yourself up for failure. It is very difficult to be with someone who is traveling down a separate path from yours.

That same fear of being alone that would convince you to stay with a man who isn't respectful of you, not trustworthy, or a combination of both, will eventually cause you to step off a godly path to keep peace or to keep that man present in your life! A little step here and a little step there and before you know it, you've totally abandoned your walk with God because you couldn't bear to be alone on Saturday night.

Make up your mind! If you are prepared to surrender your situation to Him, then surrender ALL of it. This includes the man YOU have chosen.

I know this is easier said than done. I won't try to lie to you because there are times when it feels like anyone is better than no one. But if you want God's best out of this situation—and His best is very, very good!—you're going to have to give God your best effort and work with Him.

I'm not making this up as I go along. I was a single mom living in sin with an unbeliever. Then I became a believer and he didn't. He broke my heart in so many pieces that I thought it couldn't possibly be put back together. Then God sent me His choice for my life who turned out to be a believer AND a wonderful father for my children. My faith in God's ability and promise to only give me His best when I let Him choose resulted in a great miracle in my life. I AM speaking from experience.

Let Go of Your Miracle Blockers

The hardest thing I had to do in preparation for the miracle I believed God was going to give me was to let go of the things that were blocking my miracle. I avoided dating altogether because I didn't want my kids to see a revolving door of men coming in and out of our lives. I spent all my nights alone. It was very tough, but the end result was just remarkable. The miracle He gave me for my faith and persistence was magnificent! It is the foundation of everything I do today in ministry.

Who you choose to spend your intimate life with has a tremendous impact on your children. If you are living in sin, your kids will grow up thinking it is okay to live in sin, too. If you spend more time worrying about the man in your life than you do your kids, your kids are going to seek out the love they needed from you through other avenues. Very often this means sacrificing their purity at a very young age because they are misinterpreting "sex" for love. This is not God's will for you or for your children, but only you can make the choice to switch tracks and head toward His will and His answers for your situation.

If you have been in multiple failed relationships; if you feel like every time you meet a new man he is "the one," only to have everything end with more heartbreak; if you are longing for someone to reciprocate the love you have in your heart, listen to me and listen closely.

The longing in your heart can only be filled by the Lord. Once you have let Him in and are content with Him, He will then complete the picture and fill the empty place in your heart. If He knows you are ready for the special man He has chosen to respectfully love and appreciate you, He will send you a helper who will stand by you and help you raise your family. He'll send a man who knows that His presence is the most necessary component to your successful and blessed relationship.

If He knows you are not ready for another relationship, nothing will go right. If you won't surrender to the Lord and let Him heal you, then this cycle could go on for years. It's your choice. So stopping chasing the man (or men) you hope might be *the one* who will take you away from being single. Stop sacrificing your children for the sake of "love" in all the wrong forms. No man is worth losing your kids to the world. No MAN!

Setting the Stage for Your Miracle

In the meantime, start setting the stage. A single mom needs human help as well as heavenly help, and a perfect way to start developing a help system is to find a good church home for you and your children. If you are going to church already and they are the "missing piece" to your little family and are guiding you properly through God's Word, then good for you! If you are without a church, start looking for one. Ask God to show you where He wants you and your children to worship Him.

This is another opportunity for prayer. He will guide you until you find the right church, and you'll KNOW it's the right one. By surrounding yourself and your kids with other Christians and Christian youth, you are paving the way for the most stable foundation in your children's lives. You'll also start to realize God's will for marriage and intimate relationships through the proper teaching of God's Word. A good church home is a gift to be embraced.

A single mom can protect her kids the same way two parents can together. This is where the resources I make available to you on my website not only will come in handy, but they will become a necessity in the protection you are setting up for your kids. You can take the steps I've outlined for you and utilize the software I will list for you.

Never forget that a single mom's kids are exposed to the same sex-saturated world that married moms' kids are exposed too. The exposure will have the same effect, but the actions you take to teach and guide your children will make all the difference in the world.

If you're one of the thousands and thousands of women who wonder if God's plan for you might not involve a life partner, let me briefly touch on this issue. I believe that God gives us the ability to love so much that when that love is rejected or not reciprocated, our hearts break to the point of bringing our lives almost to a standstill. There is no doubt that love is God's greatest gift to us and when it is appreciated and nurtured the way we are meant to appreciate and nurture it, it inspires us to be the best we can be.

Love for God, love for our significant others, love for our kids and family and friends make life worth living. But I am often fearfully asked, "But what if God doesn't mean for me to have anyone to love or to share my life with?"

My answer to that is that so long as you're moving into a right relationship with the Lord and the longing for a life partner to love remains in your heart, keep praying for God's best choice for you. For the few women I have met along the way who really were meant to be single, their longing for a husband turned into a joyous longing to serve the Lord. If this is the path for you, you will be blessed in ways you have never known if you follow it. It will be a plan that will be exciting, filling you with great contentment and peace while serving God.

Since not all women are cut out for this plan, I believe that God will have a special someone for those women who really do long for a life partner and are willing to accept His choice. I can assure you that His choice will be so much better than anyone you could choose for yourself. I hope you will find the faith and the ability to trust Him while you wait on His best for you, believing that He truly knows who and/or what will make you the happiest, the most fulfilled, and the best you can be. You will KNOW when His ultimate blessing for your life has manifested.

Take it one step at a time. Rome wasn't built in a day. You can find resources in the last chapter and on my website that will help you further deal with some of these issues, especially the "soul mate" issue. I've made a special effort to cover all the things we've talked about in this chapter, and you'll find special lessons and steps on dealing with the things we've only touched on when you get on my site.

Single Mom Section of My Website

The Single Mom's section of my site is interactive which means that you don't have to work through the tough decisions alone. There are others who are going through the same thing as you, as well as trained coaches who will guide you. Make it a regular stop on your daily travels, and we'll get through the single mom situations together until your miracle manifests!

P.S. AVOIDING MISTAKES THAT MANY SINGLE MOMS MAKE

Here is a list of some of the most common mistakes single moms can make with their ex- husbands, the men who just happen to be the fathers of their children. See if you think that you might be a couple of inches over the line into any of these categories and then think about what you can do about it.

"Welfare Check" Gone Bad—Dad calls to check on the welfare of the kids or talk to them, and you answer the phone. Don't use his call as an opportunity to begin complaining and take him on a guilt trip that ends up turning a phone call meant for good for the kids into a big fight. You'll get upset and angry, he'll get upset and angry, and your kids will end up bearing the brunt of it. You owe your kids more than a visit or conversation with Dad that starts off with so much negativity. If your ex is trying to be a part of their lives, let him!

Making Life Impossible—Dad wants to spend time with the kids, but no matter when he tries to arrange it, it's not convenient for you. The feeling of being left out of the family unit you once were a part of can cause you to act in ways that make it impossible for the family unit to exist at all. If your ex is trying to make an effort to be a good dad, LET HIM! Your kids still need their dad in their life. If the circumstances you and their father have created have left them with only this option to see him ... for now do what is best for the kids.

One-Sided War—Whether you are the "leaver" or the "leavee" in your broken relationship with your children's father, he is still their FATHER. Don't badmouth their dad, don't tell them the intimate details of the dissolution, don't share all of his sins and mistakes with them, and don't paint him out to be the bad guy! *Even if he is*, this is not your kids' fault. Don't make them carry the burden of your "beef" with their dad.

Cutting Off Your Nose to Spite Your Face—Don't make a hassle out of everything from a simple phone call to setting up a visitation schedule. If your ex pays support AND he always sends gifts on birthdays and holidays, don't slip into the "if I have to suffer, everyone else has to as well" mode. He will take the path of least resistance after awhile and quit trying. You do not have the right to interfere with his attempts to be a good dad unless he is putting the children in harm's way. Harm's way does NOT include introducing them to his new girlfriend (no matter how much you dislike her), but it does include drug use, abuse, neglect, etc.

10

When Pornography Invades Your Marriage

The Invasion

One of the worst things you can experience in life is to be betrayed by someone you deeply love. This betrayal can come in many different forms, but one of the fastest growing and most heartbreaking forms of this kind of betrayal is porn addiction.

This type of betrayal isn't like a physical breaching of your trust such as your spouse acting out physical expressions of lust with another human being. It is a deeper breaching of the emotional trust that your love has been built upon for another person. In the wake of this particular situation, you find heartbreak, embarrassment, despair, and grief of a kind that you have not known before.

You are now reading a book that can transform your heart and help you cooperate with God's restoring of your relationship (allowing Him to make it even better than it was before!). These pages can help you change your thinking so that you can become the person you didn't know you could be (and I mean this in a GOOD way). When the steps in this book are properly and consistently applied to your issues, you will position yourself to receive the miracle you're desperately seeking. Get ready, because your life and relationship are about to change!

You may be too embarrassed to tell anyone that there is pornography in your spouse's life. I understand. If you have told others, I imagine you've found out that it's not easy to get practical, meaningful advice from family and friends on this matter. My most un-favorite piece of advice is: "You should just forget about him and move on." Or, "Don't worry, there are plenty of other fish in the sea," is another common platitude you might receive from well-meaning friends and family.

This is probably the last thing you want to hear at a time like this. You have just discovered that your spouse is on vacation in "Pornutopia" with a bimbo named "Pornelope," and the people you would normally turn to for help want you to go fishing or just move on.

Let's choose "moving on" with your journey to wholeness. I won't lie to you and tell you that it will all be easy; many times it will be tough. But I will tell you it will be worth it, even with the changes that you are going to have to make in your own life. Anytime you are dealing with change of any kind, it's difficult to step out of your comfort zone and travel a path you've never traveled before. And this is a journey of change.

Ask yourself again, "Is he really worth it?" If any part of you feels the pain that comes from still loving the one who betrayed you, then part of you still believes he's worth it.

I Think I Had a Nightmare!

So, let's take a hypothetical trip back in time. You decided to surprise him with a wonderful, candlelit, romantic dinner for two followed by a night of romance unlike anything since your honeymoon. You sent your kids to Grandma's house, and you chose what you would wear and wouldn't wear. Then you fired up the computer and prepared to search your recipe database for the perfect romantic dinner recipes. Instead, you found a folder packed full of images of naked women and couples in obscene situations.

Or, perhaps you rolled over in the middle of the night to cuddle with your sweetie only to discover that his side of the bed was empty. Thinking he might have gotten up for a drink of water or to use the bathroom, you waited patiently for him to return. Thirty minutes later, he still wasn't back. Wondering if he might have fallen in, you got out of bed and set out on a rescue mission. On your way down the hall, you noticed his office light shining under the door.

You thought that perhaps he just couldn't sleep and wondered if a nice back rub and a warm glass of milk might help. Mustering up all the wifely concern you could find in the wee hours of the morning, you quietly opened the door. The sight of your husband typing something to a stark-naked woman in a video chat room slammed you like a mule's kick to your stomach. For an instant, you frantically hoped you were just having a nightmare.

In the split second it took for him to realize that you were standing behind him, you were able to catch a few words of his last typed statement to this total stranger he was "talking" to. What you saw devastated you, and the first thought that came to your mind was, He's cheating on me!

Or, maybe you were putting a new dust ruffle on your bed and discovered his stash of *Hustler* magazines under the mattress.

Or maybe you happened to get to the telephone bill before he did and realized that someone in your household had been calling phone-sex numbers.

The most common discovery of porn in the home involves spouses. However, know that it might also be one of your teens. So be careful here about accusations. But whatever form of porn you've discovered, the initial shock is always the same. It's a feeling of betrayal and an instant loss of trust in the person you have given your love to.

Assuming at this point in this book that it was your spouse, let's continue in that vein. You think to yourself, Who is this person? How long has he been doing this? Has he cheated on me physically? Is he personally involved with these women online? Does he wish he could be with someone like that instead of me? What's wrong with me? Am I too fat? Not sexy enough? Not adventurous enough in the bedroom?

The most common question that hits next is: Why am I not enough? This is the person who has given you those "warm fuzzies" since the day you met him and knew he was going to be *the one* you wanted to spend forever with. Aren't I pretty enough, sexy enough, a good enough wife, or did I fail him in some other way?

You always thought that if you had a mortgage, a dog, and 2.5 kids, then your life was about as good as it gets. Toss in some good friends, a close family, and a good social life—you had the American Dream! Then, in an instant, your discovery leaves you wondering if your whole life together has been a dirty lie. The next question that hits is, What will my friends and my family think if they find out?

These initial reactions you may have after the discovery of pornography in your life are not that much different than if you had caught your spouse in the physical act of cheating. Special feelings, emotions, and intimate thoughts that are sacred to a marriage have been violated and exploited by a very powerful evil. Your feelings will churn and boil, scalding your very being. Your head keeps shouting, Why? Why?

Getting a God-Ready Heart

Do you want to give up and get out at this point? Or do you love the person who has brought you to this point too much to bail without a fight? The "force" that keeps you loving this man in spite of what you have just learned is God's way of keeping you on track when everything suddenly looks so bad.

God believes in relationships that hang together for the long haul. Think about it, He never gives up and pulls out of relationship with you each time you commit a sin or transgression. If He did, we'd all be in really deep trouble. But He loves us too much for that.

In most cases you would go to the ends of the earth for the ones you love. You would sacrifice your own personal needs many times over for them without it even feeling like it was a sacrifice; you would simply feel good to give your loved ones nice things and to do nice things for them. But it's a horrible and lonely feeling when you have given so much of yourself and your heart and then you find out that your spouse has found his own pleasures with someone else, someone he is actually paying to make him feel good!

Getting a God-ready heart for this journey will help you be inspired to draw closer to Him during the dark times. The dark times usually seem to come on nights and weekends. But in a situation involving porn addiction, there are dark times every time your loved one goes near a computer or leaves the house. The enemy will always be whispering in your ear that he is going to a strip club, that he is out with someone else, or that he has mentally and emotionally abandoned you to satisfy his pleasures in ways he doesn't feel you can.

God is the only one who can comfort you during these times. Truly trusting His promise that He will never leave nor forsake you should make the dark times more bearable. Knowing that you can close your eyes and run into your Father's arms for comfort is really all you need right now. While you're there, make sure you give Him your burdens. Tell Him what's hurting the most just the way you would tell your best friend. He wants to hear you say this because saying it to Him can help you begin to give it to Him.

One of the things I did when I was going through my darkest times was to close my eyes and imagine what God's face looked like. Some days the pain would be so bad, I would get on my knees and lay my head on the edge of my bed and just imagine it was God's lap. I would pour my heart out to Him, and I would feel calm and at peace after I did. It was as if He was really there, stroking my hair and patting my back; it was as if He was letting me know it was going to be okay.

In order to really understand God and what He is all about (which ultimately reveals what He is capable of doing in this situation), you have to regularly read His promises. The Bible has been accused of being boring and outdated. NOT TRUE! The promises that are contained within those pages and the look they give you into God's heart when you're ready for it are simply amazing. One of the first promises found in the Bible that inspired me to dig deeper is Hebrews 11:1, "*Now faith is being sure of what we hope for and certain of what we do not* (yet) *see*" (NIV).

This is saying that faith is my spiritual right to the possession of all good things that I hope for. In my case, it wasn't a man I was actually hoping for when I began to totally turn to God (even though I thought it was); I was really hoping for true love, the real thing. God knew that. When I went to find that promise, I found TONS of promises that applied to God wanting to fulfill my need to be truly loved.

Get yourself a good study Bible that you can read easily. I use a NIV (*New International Version*). It is easier to read than the *King James Version*, although I keep a KJV close by for cross-referencing. A good study Bible will explain what certain passages mean in plain English. Reading my Bible literally propelled me into God's waiting arms.

Knowing more about Him, knowing Him better, is the greatest gift you will receive on this journey because once you begin to really know Him, you realize that He will be with you forever, in everything! How awesome is that? So what's the catch? I wouldn't call living right a catch. I would just call it "finally getting your living right" and having His help and blessings on every side of you.

Here comes another promise: "*The effectual fervent prayer of a righteous man availeth much*" (James 5:16, KJV). The word "righteous" as used here means acting in accord with divine or moral law, conforming to or living by a standard of right behavior. So many people live their lives according to what society allows: out of wedlock, in fornication, being promiscuous, abusing drugs and alcohol, being dishonest, and the list goes on.

Too often we accept this way of life simply because that's what surrounds us every day. That doesn't make it right. A great deal of what is done around us is not right, but we do it too, and we allow others to do it. There isn't anything righteous about any of it. Ah, but when the bottom falls out of someone's life, suddenly the person looks up and asks God, "Why?" Interesting.

Here is another place where you have a choice. You can make a right choice, or you can make the choice that the world expects you to make. The way I see it, the things of the world are what brought you to this point in the first place. If you're going to continue to do more things the same way you have been doing them, it will be much harder to find your way again.

Should You Just Move to a Desert Island?

You don't have to lock yourself in a bomb shelter to avoid making wrong choices regarding the things in the world. It isn't necessary for you to start home-schooling your kids just to remove them from the things of the world. Living right simply means that when you are faced with the options to do something righteously or do it worldly, you have to make the right choice. You might not want to choose God's way because you think it will be boring. Ha! God's ways are never boring if you truly commit to them.

Just recently, Pastor Tom told us, "There is nothing boring about sin. Give the devil his due; he knows how to do his work. He should know; he's been doing that work for six thousand years—the same tactics over and over— AND they still work for him. Those of us in the Church, now we know how to bore people; the devil never bores with his temptations."

Meet Allison (not her real name). Ali came to *Just4ladies* holding her heart in her hands with her life shattered around her feet. Her live-in boyfriend of three years had recently left her for another woman, but he still continued to visit her occasionally to enjoy a physical relationship with her. Believing that by continuing the sexual part of their relationship he would eventually come back to her, she allowed herself to be used.

Ali was not married to him, but many married women whose husbands have left them continue to do the same thing she was doing. They allow themselves to be used by their husbands who have left them for sex in hopes that they will decide they still want their wives. In far too many cases, the truth is the man just couldn't find anybody else to sleep with that night.

Allison was devastated when her former boyfriend's new girlfriend found out about his frequent visits to Allison's house and gave him an ultimatum: either stop seeing Allison altogether or she would dump him. The new girl made twice as much money, had a nicer place to live, and in Allison's eyes, was prettier than she was. It's not hard to figure out what he chose to do.

The new girlfriend was also a stripper at an upscale men's club in the Los Angeles area. How many men have had fantasies of being with a stripper? This is a distorted fantasy that has cost hundreds of men their relationships and marriages.

Throughout their relationship this man cheated on Allison numerous times, used her for her paycheck, verbally and mentally abused her, and basically contributed nothing but his occasional company. He only visited Allison occasionally to pacify her when she confronted him about not spending enough time with her. He was just waiting for something better to come along.

Allison was so devastated by his actions that she felt she couldn't go on any longer. She felt that God had dealt her a bad hand. Even though she wasn't regularly practicing her faith, she did believe in God's ability to fix her world. On one hand she was blaming God, but on the other she was claiming she believed that God could restore her relationship. Do you see the inconsistency of that?

She could not believe that God could be allowing this situation to happen to bring her back to where she needed to be in her faith—closer to Him and safe in His love for her. Her general attitude was that God was forsaking her in allowing this breakup to occur, BUT maybe if she prayed hard enough, she could get God to bring him back. What Allison wanted was the restoration of an obviously unhealthy relationship steeped in sin. So she came to me asking me to stand for her relationship with this guy to be healed and restored. She asked me to pray that he would come back, and I promised her I would pray for God's perfect will.

During our first conversation, I asked Allison what she loved about this man. I asked her to tell me what she missed about the relationship. Her response was that he was nice to her in the beginning, he used to buy her candy, and he sometimes took her out to eat.

"How long ago was this?" I asked.

"Back when we first started dating," she admitted. She went on to explain that he had lost his job shortly after that and that when he did, she offered to let him move into her place. This all happened within three months of their meeting. They lived together for almost three years during which time he contributed very little to the relationship, either emotionally or financially. Allison didn't care. She was not alone; that's all that mattered to her.

To make matters worse, Allison and her guy regularly smoked pot which she bought. They experimented with various other drugs on a "social level," and a few times had even gone so far as to get involved with a swingers' crowd. This is when couples swap partners for hours or even a night. Allison thought that she simply couldn't live without him.

This was a no-brainer situation. You don't even need to be an "experienced" Christian to see how far off base her prayer request was for God to restore this relationship!

Allison continued to party with her friends, and to smoke pot on the weekends. And when she got really lonely, she visited her swinger friends. All during this time she was extremely upset that God was not responding to her prayer that He would restore her relationship with this man. She believed that He could do anything, so why wasn't He doing it for her?

Does it seem that God isn't answering your prayers the way you think He should? Pastor Tom gives us some good insight on this.

Note from Tom: God answers every prayer He hears, but sin in the heart of the praying person can keep the prayer from being answered the way the person is hoping for (read Psalms 66:17-19).

God answers every prayer that He hears. Sometimes He answers "No." Our problem is that we want every prayer to be answered "Yes." That just won't happen until we learn how to pray for His will in every issue of our lives.

Sometimes He answers, "Wait awhile," which frustrates us.

You wonder if you believed harder, could you get what you want? The devil believes in God; in fact, he's been right there in front of God's Throne in heaven (Job 1:6; 2:1) for centuries. He hasn't had to take God's existence by "faith." Thinking that if you could only have a face-to-face talk with God, He would see things your way won't work, either. Satan's been face to face with God for centuries, and God isn't giving him what he wants.

Believing in Him or having a have a face-to-face chat with Him won't be enough for you to get what you're asking WHEN you are asking for a wrong answer. You need to be asking for God's will, for His perfect answer, and you need to believe that He wants to give you that answer. You need to have faith in His goodness and faithfulness to you. He won't give you something that will perpetuate your sinning and your pain, no matter how hard you pray or how much you say you believe in Him.

Probably everyone has heard the illustration of the man pushing the wheelbarrow across Niagara Falls on a high wire, but it really illustrates the point I'm trying to make here. Over and back he went, over and back, pushing that wheelbarrow. At each return, he would ask if the people believed that he could cross the falls again while pushing the wheelbarrow. "Oh, yes," they would say. "Yes, we believe you can do it."

"Do you really believe?" he'd ask, and the people would adamantly reply that they did. "Then," he finally replied, "come over here and get in this wheelbarrow and go with me."

No takers! They really didn't believe, did they?

I brought the subject of Allison's pot smoking habit up to her. Her response was that God made pot, so why would He be upset if she was smoking it? Ugh!

Approaching the throne of God with a situation you are caught up in that you truly want to rid yourself of is one thing. God will help you if you are ready to let Him. But to approach Him with a request that is absolutely ungodly while you refuse to give up the sin you are involved in is a surefire way to hear silence on the other end. The Bible says this, *"I cried out to him with my mouth; his praise was on my tongue. If I had cherished sin in my heart, the Lord would not have listened"* (Psalm 66:17-18, NIV).

You need to learn to filter out those things that you may have been justifying as okay with God, when they are not. You need to stand firm on new godly standards and start making righteous choices every day. This isn't a case of God trying to force you to be righteous so that you can *earn* the promise of an answer if you do—this is a case of God not answering you when you are being unrighteous and hanging on to your sin. If you are trying to let go of your sin and you want to hear what God is telling you, God is hearing every word you say!

James Bond or Snoopy?

When you suspect your loved one of experimenting with porn, it's your natural instinct to want to go through everything he owns to find proof of it. This includes the car, the computer, his office, the garage, his wallet, nightstand drawers, and any other place where he might try to hide it. This can be an obsession to find the porn he has an obsession with, when in reality, you're forming a compulsive/obsessive behavior yourself. You're becoming addicted to finding proof so you can confront him, but every discovery you make only hurts you more. Don't do it.

Some would question why I'm saying that it is okay to invade the privacy of your child, but you should not invade your husband's private areas.

My response to that is that your children are your RESPONSIBILITY; it is up to you to protect them from the evils that can creep into their world. Although there is a certain amount of trust that has to be given, you are still the parent. You are supposed to know better when they don't, and you are supposed to protect them from many things, including evil influences.

Marriage involves the joining together of two equals. It's not your responsibility to teach your spouse right from wrong except through the indirect influence of watching you make right choices and watching how you live your life. What about in-his-face teaching of right from wrong? That's God's job! Trust plays a major part in marriage and when it's violated, it's up to the couple to rebuild that trust one piece at a time. Searching a spouse's belongings may be the most common way to discover his indiscretions, but this behavior can also devastate your hopes of ever learning to trust again.

Even if your loved one is telling you that he has given it up and he isn't doing it anymore, but you KNOW he is, focusing on discovering proof to confirm this will never be constructive. The fact is, your response to the discovery will only cause him to shut you out more. There has to come a point where you realize you ARE NOT responsible for the actions he is taking, and your discovery of proof of his addiction WILL NOT make him change. Changing your attitudes and your actions, however, can strongly influence him to want to change.

The hurt you feel when you do find the pornography will set you back spiritually more than you know. The first thing that will usually come to your mind is, "I am praying and have faith that God will fix this; so why am I still finding it?"

If your focus is on the substance of his addiction, you will find that you bring it up in every fight or disagreement you have. Women who are losing an argument or not getting the response they want will fall back on pulling out transgressions from fifteen years past. Men are usually amazed at our ability to remember very single word they have ever uttered to us, good and bad, since the day we first met.

Add the more recent incident of his pornography addiction, and you have the makings of a divorce in every argument you choose to have with him. Even though he isn't saying it, he is feeling shame, embarrassment, and even remorse for the hold this vice has on him. When you throw gasoline on those smoldering coals, you're bound to get an explosion that will take a longer time to extinguish.

The best thing you can do is to recondition your thinking. This will be a long-term reconditioning, so be ready for the enemy to dangle lack of progress in front of you every time your spouse either does or doesn't do something that displeases you.

Just4Ladies member Mandy (not her real name) came to us in a rage. Her husband of thirty years was going through what she believed was a mid-life crisis. She loved him so much that it was killing her to stand by while he raced around in his new Mazda Miata, wore clothing made for a twenty-year-old, changed his hairstyle, and even started wearing cologne, something he hadn't done since their wedding day thirty years prior.

Mandy was convinced that her husband was having an affair, and all of his actions truly pointed in that direction. The *Just4Ladies* prayer angels she contacted convinced her to calm down and take it one day at a time. She needed proof before she could confront him. She was still too angry to just be devastated and defeated at that point, an inevitable feeling that would come sooner or later.

So she decided to document his behavior and any late nights at work, unplanned trips out of town, suspicious charges on the credit card statements, etc. Surprisingly, Dan came home like clockwork every night. He never stayed at the office late, and the few times he had trials that kept him after regular business hours, a trip by the courthouse proved he was where he said he was.

What was even more bizarre was that he was acting like a teenage boy in their intimate life as well. At first she thought it was just a surge in testosterone or some "guy thing" that happens when men go through a mid-life crisis. "It wasn't that it was bad, it was just not him," Mandy said. "He was treating me like I wasn't a lady. He never did that before. He was always very respectful and romantic, always a gentleman in bed."

Instead of discovering that he was having an affair like she fully expected, she discovered that he was spending his evenings in online chat rooms. Dan accidentally left himself signed on to the computer while he took a business call, and Mandy happened to be looking for something in their study when she made this discovery. She was floored when she read the chat line he was exchanging with a girl young enough to be his daughter.

Without saying a word, Mandy left the study and waited until Dan left to go to the office the next day. She signed onto his screen name and began going through his online "stuff" with a fine-tooth comb. Each discovery tore out another piece of her heart. All the online chat ladies Dan had bookmarked were in their early twenties. Did he want a young girl? After all, she was in her early fifties and not nearly as attractive as she had once been, at least not in her eyes.

To Mandy's knowledge, Dan had never physically met any of these women, but the fact that he was talking to them via a Web cam seemed almost as bad. Mandy became obsessed with gathering as much "evidence" as she could for the confrontation of a lifetime. Dan had no idea what he was in for. Neither did Mandy.

Mandy didn't stop at the computer. She went through everything he owned, including his workshop out in the garage. She found numerous adult magazines and a few advertisements for phone-sex lines. Confrontation day came and it was ugly. Dan came home from work and after supper retired to the study to do some legal research, or so he said. Mandy, armed with a pile of porn, crashed through the door, threw it down on the desk, and proceeded to literally come unglued.

Dan tried to explain that he was just trying to get "stimulated" for her and that it wasn't hurting anyone if he just talked to these women over the computer. He tried to justify it with the fact that he had never met any of them nor had intentions of meeting them. After a terrible fight, Dan agreed to stop. But Mandy continued to dig and search and spy. She didn't trust Dan to stick to his promise, which was understandable after what had happened—even if it was a big mistake on her part.

Overexposing the Issue

Mandy's actions continually netted her more finds. Later she did realize that most of the stuff she discovered was from before her confrontation and his promise to give it up. But this didn't stop her from accusing Dan and fighting with him about it again.

After three weeks of fighting, Dan decided to leave for a while, thinking it would be best for them to spend some time alone. Mandy was devastated by his decision and was convinced he was either going to meet one of his "cyber bimbos" or divorce her. She complained that he never even made an effort to try to fix the situation. She felt she was justified in her spy program and insisted that any woman would have done the same.

Here is where Mandy went wrong. After her confrontation, Dan felt extreme shame for what he had been doing. Dan expressed his feelings and admitted to Mandy with an open heart that it had made him feel young again and it did stimulate him, but he knew that it was wrong. This was the exact response Mandy wanted from him, and she should have laid the anger down right there and started rebuilding their trust.

Instead, she allowed the obsession of trying to find more and more to hold against him to fuel her anger and sense of outrage. Ultimately, her obsession cost her several months of her marriage. It wasn't her job to monitor Dan's every movement at that point; it was her job to begin trying to trust him again and to encourage him to do what he knew he had to do. By becoming a live-in spy, she pushed him out the door.

When we talked about her actions, she was indignant. "Well, look at what HE did! I had a right to be that way!" Two wrongs never make a right. In Mandy's marriage, someone needed to make a move toward starting to repair the damage that had already been done, not creating more. When you've asked God into your situation, you have to let Him take the reins. Ruling by rage or the assumption that you deserve to get even is not a recipe for a repaired marriage.

Finally, after several months of anger, hate, and rage (none of which come from *Above*), Mandy was ready to get serious about rebuilding her marriage. She finally meant it when she asked God to soften her heart and help her forgive. Forgiveness is always a required element of marriage restoration. As with the Lord, we have to imitate what He does. We have to forgive and then wipe the slate clean.

Dan came back, but a lot had changed between them. Mandy took her focus off the porn and the possibility that he was looking at it, and she started focusing on getting through each day by trusting God. She focused on her actions and her attitude toward Dan and how they would affect the way he treated her or responded to her. Some days it was one hour at a time because the temptation to spy on Dan was overwhelming. She knew it was up to Dan, however, through her prayers and support, to overcome the addiction.

He did overcome. The ending to their story was happy, but the road they took to that happy ending was a lot of hard, hard work.

Spying Won't Help

If your spouse is caught up in pornographic websites or others means of using porn, you can spy all you want. Confronting your spouse with your discoveries and your anger can definitely make him feel more guilt, shame, and remorse than he already does. This will sometimes cause men to do what men do when they feel they are in a no-win situation: they simply leave.

The other thing he might do is move his access to this pleasure-giving material to a location that he is sure you won't find out about it—maybe at work or at a friend's house. The bad thing about this is that most employers will fire an employee who is accessing porn on company computers. You don't need that either. At this stage, what may be a controllable problem at home or just a curiosity can spiral violently out of control and become a true addiction.

Here is how most men think in a situation like this: The only escape from the shame and embarrassment of their addictive actions is to avoid being confronted. The only way they may see to avoid being confronted is to remove their addiction to a place where they can't be confronted. This is the LAST thing we want them to do.

So what am I supposed to do, tolerate it? I'm sure you're asking. Tolerating something means you put up with it. This is a question that doesn't have an easy answer. First you have to look at a few things like are there children or teens in your home? If so, tolerating porn or putting up with it is NOT an option. If your spouse is unable to realize this, you have to be able to take more drastic measures.

If you are afraid that laying down the law about pornography in your home will cause your spouse to leave, please take a moment to think about the effects pornography will have on your children if they should happen across it. Most mothers say they wouldn't risk exposing their kids to that for anyone or anything. But in today's society, more and more mothers are willing to sacrifice what is best for their kids in order to accommodate what they think is best for themselves.

Keeping their men in the home is far more important to them than eradicating the porn. Not being alone overrides the instincts that most mothers have to protect their children at all costs. This is a dangerous way to think and can produce terrible consequences. The bottom line is that porn is porn and it's very evil. Do what you have to do to remove the evil from your home. It isn't going to change and become non-destructive. It is bad, it's always been bad, and it will always be bad.

Put Up with Him, But Don't Ever Make Your Kids Put Up with Porn

Putting up with a spouse who is addicted to porn or a teen who is experimenting with porn is one thing and they may have to be "tolerated" while you wage this war. But laying down the law about the actual pornography being in your home is something for which you should fiercely stand.

Well, how do I deal with it then? is your next question, I'm sure. First, you pray about the situation. When faced with a difficult situation, call on God. He is more than willing to give you the wisdom you need to properly deal with the issue. Once you have prayed and asked for His help, be still and listen in your heart for response and guidance.

A good example of His speaking to you would be a situation where you have found pornography in your home and your initial reaction is anger and a desire to confront. Knowing now that no problem is solved in anger, you go to prayer instead. Before you know it, your anger has started dissolving and you can think a little clearer. You are not as prone to saying something you will later regret, because you've allowed the Lord to share His peace with you. In most cases, He will fill your mind with the right things to say and do. Choose to ask for and then heed His guidance.

It's necessary to watch your words and actions at this point because the consequences of them can be ugly and long-term. Once you have prayed and feel the Lord is guiding you and protecting you, calmly sit down with your spouse and say something along these lines: "I know that you know this situation is hurting me and it is damaging our relationship. But I have prayed and I have faith that you're going to do the right thing. I have faith to believe that beginning with your promise now and then your actions to match it, you will remove all of this material from our home and from our computer, and wherever else it might be so that our children do not accidentally find it."

If he promises to do so, you should ask him to do it immediately and to show you proof that it's done. Once he has, then drop it. Don't warn him not to do it at work or anywhere else; your warning isn't going to be effective anyway. Your goal in this situation is to make it clear that you will not put up with pornographic material in your home. In the event that he responds with something like this, "It's my computer and it's locked so no one can see it," or something along those lines, you can reiterate your condition of no porn in your home. Then drop it and be ready to go to plan "B."

Plan "B"

One woman I coached gave her husband this condition and after breaking his promise three times, she calmly packed a bag and loaded her kids into the car. Her husband came outside and asked where she was going, and she told him she was going to stay with her sister until she was sure it was safe for her kids to be in their house.

Her husband was appalled. No one in their family knew there was any problem, let alone that he was involved in looking at pornography. He begged her to just wait and he would do it right then. After a twenty-five minute wait in the car in the driveway, he came outside with a bag of magazines. Her inspection of the computer with porn-detecting software proved he had indeed gotten rid of it. She never raised her voice or became hateful. She simply let him know that his inability to keep his promise had caused her to take the necessary actions needed to safeguard her family from his addiction.

He never expected her to take such drastic action. She admitted later that she was dying inside at the thought of leaving her home and her husband because despite his problem, she still loved him. But she stood her ground on protecting her kids and gave him a choice of whether or not to respect that. He had no choice but to follow suit.

As much as you want to go up one side of him and down the other, muster up all your strength and walk away from an argument and an excuse for him to escape to his computer. Remember, you can only control and change yourself. He will have no choice but to change based on your actions. Keeping your focus on that and not on him or his indiscretion is the goal of this step. Take it one day at a time and sometimes one hour at a time. I've known women who have had to do it one minute at a time!

Focusing all your energy on his problem or what he is or is not doing because of the addiction leaves you little time to focus on yourself and the things you have to change. It also leaves a back door for the enemy to slip through, and slip through he will. He'll use all the little things that are bothering you to keep you focused on your spouse, which in turn will create a breeding ground for further arguments, anger, and strife that can lead to disaster.

It takes superhuman strength to tear yourself away from the root of the problem and the person who brought it into your life. A good way to deal with the temptation to stay riveted on the issue is to be aware of your thoughts because they become your actions, as you'll learn in the next chapter.

You can control where your mind wanders even if you'd rather stay focused on the negative. Sometimes it's more comfortable to do that because you almost know what to expect. It isn't easy, but you can change your focus one thought at a time. If you slip, don't worry and fret about it. Just go back to square one and start over again. The support groups that you can become involved with, which can be found with prayer groups at the end of this book, will provide the help you need when you need it the most. Utilize them. That's what they are there for.

11

Action for Reaction

Fine-Tuned Manipulation

Without a doubt, women are the ones who created the concept that I call "Action for a Reaction." This is a psychological game females play in an attempt to get a desired reaction out of their male counterparts. Men very rarely use this particular device, as it requires way too much planning and more effort than they care to put into it.

I have known some women who have planned their strategy for days and even weeks. They strategize how they are going to act, what they are going to say, and how they are going to respond when they finally say something to get the reaction they are looking for. We've all done it because we were all born with the female manipulation gene. How we use it from this point forward is the key to either more failure or more success.

This action for a reaction form of manipulation almost always backfires. I know this is true because I think I could have created the concept and entitled it: *"What to Say or Do While You're Saying What You're Going to Do That Will Really Screw Things Up Beyond Repair or Recognition."* I'll have to talk to my publisher about that being my next book because I am sure it would be a best seller.

The most common responses to the discovery of your spouse's involvement with pornography involve several steps. First you are devastated to the point of tears and shock. Then you ask the "Do you wish you could be with someone like that?" question.

That question is almost always followed by this answer, "No! Of course not! The Website just popped this up in front of me and curiosity got the best of me." Never mind the fact that you've learned that he has been the *victim* of accidental porn pop-up trails to these Websites for the last nine months, accidents that curiosity just forced him to look at.

Or there is the macho response, "I'm a guy. I'm supposed to look. When I quit looking, I'm dead."

To which you probably would think to yourself, Not yet, honey; but while we're on that subject, why don't you go and take a little nap?

Dangerous R&R: Rage Reaction

The next common reaction is rage. For you quiet types, this might just be "extreme anger." I'm Italian, so I fall into the rage category. You can't wait till he gets home so you can scratch his eyes out. Then you plan to beat him with the closest object not tied down, preferably the computer monitor he was using when he had his little "accidents." The next few hours are spent simmering in your own acidic juices while you wait for him to get home. God help him if he comes through the door and asks what's for dinner.

Next the disgust sets in. This is the part where you look at the man you have been madly in love with for however long and you feel like heaving. You think about what he has done to you, your family, and your way of life. All for some nekkid (southern for *no clothes on*) bimbo who was charging him $4.99 per minute to tell him things she was reading out of a Jackie Collins novel.

After several repeat performances of this drama, the effect wears out. And one day you realize that he is no longer begging or groveling at your feet, and he isn't bringing home flowers or jewelry any more. That must mean that he's back talking to his over-priced cyber-bimbo again, right?

You instantly begin thinking about what you can say or do to make him keep showing how sorry he is. This is the "Action for Reaction" strategy and it functions on many levels. You start off with the "mild" level. As he keeps getting used to each level, you work your way up to the "extreme" level. The worst part about this is that you really do not mean the threats that you are making and you have no intention of carrying them out. You simply want to find a level where you can get him to react the way you want him to.

This is manipulation. The definition of *manipulate* is "to control or play upon by artful, unfair, or insidious means—especially to one's own advantage." When you have reached the "I want a divorce!" action/threat stage, hoping he is going to start the begging and groveling reaction, you've gone too far. All you really wanted him to do is beg and grovel; you are at threatening divorce and wondering how you got there.

"Action for Reaction" is a self-gratifying tool of manipulation. It never produces any long-range positive or productive results. It actually produces just the opposite result. This form of manipulation manages to insert resentment into the situation, and resentment is one item that is tough to get rid of. If you don't have it, don't get it. If you do have it, do whatever you have to do to get and stay rid of it.

I know that the hardest thing to do can be to just stand by and do nothing. When your loved one does not respond to your feelings, those raw emotions almost always begin to seek ways to make him respond. This will never produce the reaction you're hoping for, because real life just doesn't work like it does in the movies or in the books.

In real life when a man feels cornered, he will attack back or he will retreat to a place where he doesn't have to deal with it. Forcing him to deal with it isn't a solution. It all goes back to the "you can't change anyone but you" theory. So what are you expected to do?

You're expected to hold yourself accountable for your part in what happens from the point you discovered the pornography forward. You can allow your emotions to rule your actions which will result in a negative outcome, or you can turn to the Lord and ask Him for the strength you need to overcome the temptation to cut loose on your spouse. As far as you have come in your journey, what do you think God would have you do?

Your Own God Book Journal

A very good way to help you deal with your frustration is to start a journal. Keeping a diary is a reasonable and safe way to release pent-up emotions. I call my journal my *God Book*. I write what I need to say to Him in my God Book every day. I'll admit that some days I am angry and some days I am at peace. Either way, when I've said what I felt I needed to say in my God Book, I don't have to spew it out on whoever is driving me up the wall. He knows how to deal with me when I feel that way.

"God-Booking" is also a good way to communicate your frustration to the Lord. When you go back and read what you have written from the beginning, you will be amazed at how far you have come and how many temptations you have avoided. You can always find God listening when you're in your God Book.

One woman I came to know through *Just4Ladies* was about midway in her journey. Linda (not her real name) had discovered her husband's porn addiction about three months before I met her and she had been applying the methods she found in my first book, *A Course in Heartbreak*. She had basically dealt with all of the above and was doing quite well. She was determined to trust God for the outcome and came to us for some extra support.

During the second month of her journey, she moved out of the bedroom she shared with her husband. This shocked him a little, but he was hooked on a video chat girl and was actually contemplating relocating to Las Vegas to be with her.

In her testimony, Linda shared with us how her heart felt like it was being ripped from her chest when he told her that he was thinking about leaving, but she held her composure and told him she loved him enough to stand by him and help him with this problem. She made it clear, however, that if he chose to leave her for this other woman, she would move on and there would be no second chances.

She informed him that she was moving into their guest bedroom to give him some space and time to think about what he was doing. Linda shared with us how she lay in bed each night and cried herself to sleep. She missed her husband and the closeness they had shared. "We had never slept without at least one part of our bodies touching each other. We always slept close and cuddled. It was my favorite time of the day when I could crawl into bed and just be next to him all safe and sound and warm," Linda recalled.

"I knew that when he started coming to bed hours after I had fallen asleep and was staying on the opposite side that I was losing him to this evil. I tried to lie close to him one night and he jumped out of bed and started yelling at me to give him some space and not smother him. For twelve years he had no problem with this, usually meeting me in the middle. Now I was *smothering* him. I was so hurt."

It was that night that Linda lay awake until long after her husband had started snoring, and prayed that God would save their marriage. She was determined to do it completely by His Book, knowing that God's Word was truth and He could not lie. She knew enough to know that He only needed her to do her part, which was to hold back her anger and her emotions and, as calmly as possible, let Him do His work. So she did.

In Matthew 6:33-34, God's Word tells us, *"Seek first his kingdom and his righteousness, and all these things will be given to you as well. Therefore do not worry about tomorrow, for tomorrow will worry about itself. Each day has enough trouble of its own"* (NIV).

Linda became so immersed in learning about the Lord from that point forward that the pain of her husband's addiction became easier to bear. She would come to our prayer boards and post a morning prayer and greeting. She never failed to let the other ladies know she was praying for them and more often that not, she would leave them a bit of encouragement to help them get through the day.

Then one day her husband knocked on her door and asked if he could come into her room. He sat down on the edge of her bed and began sobbing. Linda was stunned, but she asked him what the problem was. He confessed he had been a total fool and when he finally realized what a fool he had been, he was hit with the reality that the wife he had adored had drifted away from him.

He told her how he had woken up in the middle of the night and realized she wasn't touching him. He knew then and there that what he was doing was wrong and began praying to God, begging Him to give him a second chance. He never wrote the other girl to explain; he simply shut his account off, knowing she was what she was and would never mean what Linda meant to him.

He said he knew Linda didn't love him anymore because she had just stopped caring about what he was doing. She stopped catering to his every need, wasn't making him special desserts, or packing notes in his lunch. She had changed.

In reality, Linda was so determined to stay close to God in order to get past the pain she felt that she spent hours and hours each day writing in her God Book. She focused on God, and not on the problem she had agreed to surrender to Him for fixing. She was spending a lot of time praying with other women and talking to God in her book; while she was focusing on that, God was focusing on her and her problem.

Her husband sensed the change in her, felt her withdraw, and ended up changing himself as a result. Linda and her husband are now part of a wonderful church in their hometown where they lead a prayer group for troubled couples. Linda says her marriage has never been better.

Change is the hardest thing we have to do at times, but sometimes change can be very good and can work wonders to our advantage.

Run and Retreat!

Even without a thorn in your side like a spouse who is addicted to or involved in pornography, you need a special retreat spot. In order to hear the Lord and His direction for you, you have to find a quiet spot where you can meet with Him. In addition to being able to pray and meditate, your special retreat spot is a good place to go when the world feels like it is crashing around you. In war, retreat is not always bad. Retreat is good for regrouping and reorganizing and re-strategizing.

It's tough to be able to keep a cool temper, a calm disposition, and an even attitude when the kids are fighting, dinner's burning, the phone is ringing, dogs are barking, someone's knocking, and basically the world is breaking loose around you. And while all of this is going on, you realize that your spouse has locked himself in his study (his "porn chamber" as you may have started referring to it). You're no good to anyone when you're frazzled like this, including yourself.

It's time to retreat ... and fast!

My favorite spot to retreat was always by the ocean, but it wasn't easy for me to go there every day. So instead, I found a nice quiet spot out on my back patio that overlooked a few palm trees and the neighbor's pool. In the early morning hours, I went out and just listened to the sounds of morning: birds chirping, the distant hum of someone mowing their lawn, maybe the wind blowing the palm fronds. All of these things brought me closer to God. I stopped looking at life through worldly eyes and started seeing things as best as I could through His divine eyes.

He allowed me a glimpse of what I should take notice of first in life. For me, I had never taken the time to really appreciate the landscape. How many of us do unless we're avid birdwatchers or hikers? Behind all of life's problems there is an absolutely gorgeous world out there that we have been blessed with. We've forgotten that somewhere along the way.

The Lord and I spend a lot of time reading. I lie on the couch with the Bible and it is as if He shows me the things He wants me to read. I spend most of this time also praying. I feel so close to the Lord during those days. A few times I have even prayed that He would send rain just so we could spend the day together! Eventually, I learned I don't need rain to be close to Him; He is always there.

How to Establish Your Retreat Space

Time alone with God is essential to Christian growth. But the circumstances of our lives conspire to keep us busy; plus our own resistance to accepting His grace helps us find excuses to avoid this time even when it is our desire. There are several things we can do, however, to break down this resistance and create the space for our prayer life to flourish.

First, make a prayer space. This can be a room, a chair, a corner or wherever you feel most comfortable and relaxed.

Second, choose a regular prayer time. The preferable time is when you're awake and alert. Don't try to pray for twenty minutes or a half hour before bed if you're a morning person, or before your morning coffee if you're a night owl. Be as consistent as possible. Write it in your agenda if you need to. For those with children at home, finding any time alone at all may be the greatest challenge—ask God to help you. He wants to spend time with you more than you do with Him.

Get creative: Maybe everyone in your home needs to have a quiet time in the late afternoon or after dinner so that you can have yours, too. Maybe your prayer time is fifteen minutes in the school parking lot waiting for dismissal. You will probably have to steal this time from some other worthy endeavor, but remember—God time has to be a priority.

Third, make it easy for yourself to pray. This seems obvious, but I can count many times when I've made it hard by being inflexible in how I pray. I have a problem with setting overly ambitious goals for myself, a sure recipe for discouragement. Set reasonable goals that you enjoy meeting.

Don't be intimidated if you feel that you don't know how to pray; read a book or talk about how you feel to your pastor or a mature friend in faith at church. Go slowly and be gentle on yourself. Maybe you have some notions of what prayer is (or isn't) that are causing anxiety or self-doubt. Let them go. Try different methods of prayer and choose those you enjoy. If sitting still makes you fidgety, pray while taking a walk. Prayer walking is good physical and spiritual exercise, and you'll find that in the process that you're probably losing weight! Double blessing!

Fourth, explore your family traditions for prayer. If you have backslidden from church attendance, except for weddings and funerals, do a little research and see where your roots come from. I was raised Catholic, but I now attend a Southern Baptist Church. Both denominations have played key roles in my spiritual development because although they are denominations, I look beyond the borders and see the message God gives through each one. If you were raised one way and your spouse another, try both ways. In addition to this giving you a reason to re-establish yourself in a church family, it will be easier for your spouse to come when he is ready. A family that prays together really does STAY together!

Pastor Tom is a prayer expert; here's what he has to say about prayer.

Note from Pastor Tom: Solitary prayer can take many forms, but prayer is, above all, a time of intentionally attending to the presence of God. This attention and listening to God are the source of spiritual power: *"Those that wait on The Lord shall renew their strength; they shall mount up like eagles`..."* (Isaiah 40:31).

The psalmist uses the image of a resting child to describe the soul at prayer: *"But I still my soul and make it quiet, like a child upon its mother's breast; my soul is quieted within me ...* (Psalm 131:3, The Book of Common Prayer).

When we open our attention to God in quiet prayer and reflection, we allow the Spirit to restore and renew us. Through a patient commitment to this practice, we are nurtured into Christian maturity, and learn to pray with joy.

It is necessary for you to have a break from all the stuff going on around you including the issue that has brought you to the foot of the cross in the first place. In addition to your own personal retreat place, find a good church to attend. A good church is not only a blessing, but it will allow you the fellowship you need to stay rooted in the Christian walk you are taking. If feelings of shame or embarrassment are keeping you from this source of strength, don't give the enemy the satisfaction of setting you up in spiritual isolation at this time. God will help you find a church where you can feel comfortable and welcome.

Who and What is The Enemy?

Whether you were raised to believe it or knew it all along, there is good in this world and there is also great evil: the enemy, the devil, Satan, Lucifer, and a whole bunch of other names that all spell E.V.I.L. The Bible tells us all about him. Two Old Testament passages (Isaiah 14:12-15) and (Ezekiel 28:11-19) furnish a picture of Satan's original position. It's good reading and I highly recommend it.

We know that all good things come from God, but what about the things that *appear* to be good, like love or sex?

How can something be evil if it seems to be good and fills a need you have? How can you feel so much "love" for someone who might be abusive or disrespectful or not reciprocate that love? It is possible to be deceived into believing that what you have is love when in reality, and by God's standards, it isn't love at all?

Long, long ago, somewhere near the beginning of time as God set it, Lucifer (the devil)—originally an archangel in Heaven—decided he wanted to be God. The name *Lucifer* means "light giver" or "light bearer." The pride this angel had knew no bounds. You can pretty well figure out that when you are so proud of yourself that you decide to try to overthrow God, the results are going to be bad. Really bad. Lucifer found this out the hard way. His pride and arrogance got him thrown out of heaven and earned him an eternity in hell.

Lucifer was a beautiful angel. He was probably breathtaking to look at, perhaps in a Robert Redford kind of way. But he was so cocky that even after God banished him to the earth, he didn't throw in the towel. He must have thought that if he spent all his time on earth convincing as many of us as he could to spend eternity with him, he could strike back at God that way. His methods of evil deception are boundless.

Evil can often appear to be quite lovely. A good example of this is a married man who falls head over heels in love (in his mind) with another woman. What makes it even worse is when the man is a believing Christian and knows how God feels about such things. But this man meets a beautiful woman and nothing else matters. He feels the pitter-patter in his heart that convinces him it MUST be love if it feels this good.

All of his Christian training and education go flying out the window, and one day he comes home and tells his wife he is leaving because he has met *the one* for him. He explains that this woman is beautiful and nice and he loves her. On the surface, anyone listening to him would really think he was in love. To those of us who know how evil works, we know he is in *lust* and is mislabeling the word love because the enemy has blinded him to the truth.

How can love be evil? How can a beautiful and sweet woman be evil? How can sex, a natural God-given instinct and need, be evil? Real love, real beauty and sweetness, and godly sex are not evil because they are from God. But devil-inspired, human misinterpretations of true and godly things can be quite evil.

From the second you decided you were going to bring the Lord on board in your life, you unintentionally invited opposition from the dark side. This "dark side" has nothing to do with the *Star Wars* movies. So, be forewarned that Satan will try to inspire you to misinterpret many things in order to draw you away from God's ways.

God wants more than anything to see you blessed with the perfect outcome to the dilemma in which you have found yourself. He knows that in order to give you a miracle for your situation, He needs to make sure that you will always cherish and nurture the miracle gift He wants to give to you. Most importantly, He is drawing you close to Himself to show you that He is always there, and He wants you to always lean on Him in both the good times and the bad times.

He's using this journey to train you for your own mission in His service one day soon. And so, the "wait" factor that frustrates us so much enters the equation while we're being trained to reign.

Knowing when it's From God and when it's Not

During your journey you are learning all kinds of good things about God, yourself, marriage, overcoming trials, and how to be holy. You're learning how you really can't live your life without the Lord and still expect blessed results. You're also learning how to be ready to go out into the world and help others through their situations by leading them to His light.

The devil hates this. He had you right where he wanted you before with your life saturated with too much to do and not enough time to do it. Knowing far more about you than you could imagine, he is fully away of the things that will make you feel guilty. He can't read your mind, but he has been keeping records on you since the second you were born. And now he trots out the doubts and the feelings of failure and guilt.

• Maybe you weren't spending enough time with your spouse and now you're wondering if you are responsible for his "habit." That's not God; that's the devil.

• Maybe you were so busy with work and trying to make a living that you forgot to have a life. That's not God; that's the devil.

• Maybe the things that mattered most to you weren't family and marriage; maybe they were work and material things. That's not God; that's the devil.

Whatever the case may be, the devil has had you where he wanted you a great deal of the time. The happiest ending in his eyes would be for you and your spouse to split up; for you to become an exhausted, bitter, failing single parent. He would love for your kids to grow up in a broken home.

To accomplish that end, his means will always be to try to make you choose wrong paths, believe lies, and react to things around you. It's easy for you to do all those things, especially if you have neglected seeking God's guidance for your life. You need to want to be fully armed for this battle against his tricks—a spiritual battle that some call spiritual warfare.

Let me give you an example of how easily you can fall for his tricks. You're progressing on your spiritual journey, you're doing what you know you should be doing. As you are breezing through your day filled with hope and peace, just knowing that all is going to be well, suddenly a negative thought pops into your mind about your spouse.

You instantly feel the same anger and hurt you felt at the beginning.

For some reason you rationalize that God is surely outraged with a holy anger over what you have just realized and He wants YOU to do something about it. So you totally skip over the prayers that you would pray that usually chase these destructive thoughts away. You pick up the phone and call your spouse and launch a huge argument.

Your spouse, who has been amazed at how calm and serene you've been under the circumstances, is shocked and immediately gets defensive. You both say hateful things to each other, driving the wedge between you even deeper. When you hang up, you feel instant remorse for what you have done. That wasn't God; it was the enemy tripping you up.

It would be wonderful if we could finally arrive at some point in our walk with God where we are bulletproof from Satan's wiles. But while we're still in learning mode about God and His ways, every one of us can still be deceived by Satan and completely lose sight of what we've learned about discerning what's from the Lord and what's from the enemy. Quite often God allows this to teach us more about spiritual discernment.

It also helps us learn that whether everything seems to be coming up roses or not, Satan is still always lurking around looking for just the right moment to launch such a deception attack. The more you learn, the more you will catch Satan as he tries this and you will cut him off at the pass.

Confusion is the most common weapon the enemy uses against us. He uses in it all things because he knows that especially as baby Christians, or as Christians just coming back into the mix of things, we are not always sure of what is from the Lord and what isn't. We want to walk in faith, but there is always the question, Was that God? Am I doing the right thing here? lingering in the back of our minds. Here is a little chart that may help you when you're unsure.

From God

Peace – Only God can give you peace that transcends all understanding. You know that the circumstances you are in dictate that you should be feeling upset, panicky, anxious, and even fearful; instead you feel a wonderful calm envelop you. This is always God.

From The Enemy

Fear—You are afraid he is going to leave you for Pornelope. You're afraid of the outcome of the entire situation. You're afraid of the "what if's." You're afraid of what the future holds. You're afraid of what God's will might be for your situation. You're afraid that it isn't God's will for you and your husband to be together. God says this about fear in 2 Timothy 1:7, *"I didn't give you a spirit of fear, but of power, love and of a sound mind."*

In other words, your walk is now based on love. You may not know it yet, but when you asked Jesus into your heart, you instantly received the power of the Holy Spirit. This is a mighty spiritual weapon, and your journey with God will show you how to utilize and wield that weapon. Your journey polishes you and makes you able to not only understand the power given to you as a child of God, but how to release it. Wow! That's powerful!

It is good to know that a sound mind comes as we learn to trust God more and more. We are not moved by the little annoying darts the enemy shoots at us because our faith reveals their true source and what they are made of: deception and lies.

From God

Forgiveness—This can be a tough one. Learning to forgive someone who has hurt you is not an easy thing to do, and it often cannot be done on our own. That's when God is there for you; He will teach you how. I don't believe there is a human on earth who can teach us how to forgive the really hard things. This is a lesson that can only come from our Heavenly Father.

Learning to forgive can only be fully achieved after you have accepted Jesus Christ as your Lord and Savior; otherwise you are simply acting according to your flesh. You can teach yourself to forgive on a carnal level or as a good deed; true forgiveness comes only from the Spirit of Christ within you. Until your mind is renewed, until you are enlightened by His Holy Spirit, there remains a resistance, an enmity between God and you, that will govern your every decision (Romans 12:2, Titus 3:3-5).

Forgiveness is a key element in answered prayer because when your heart harbors the enemy's luggage, it is impossible for God to fit His gifts in there. I believe it is easier to forgive your significant others because you love them so much, but the devil makes it nearly impossible to forget what they have done. This always ends up bringing you back into a vicious cycle of unforgiveness.

You also need to be able to forgive yourself for any mistakes you've made, times you've lost your temper, and accusations you've thrown out.

Your sinful nature (your flesh) has a high resistance to laying offenses aside. It prefers to take on an offense and then use the negative but powerful energy that the offense brings with it in every wrong way possible. Your unrenewed mind wants to collect offenses, hold grudges, and seek its own sense of justice. Retaliation is a driving force within unrenewed minds determined to get even! Your flesh—unrenewed, unbridled, lacking illumination and understanding, prefers to be judge, jury, and executioner of the offender—even when that offender is your own self.

From The Enemy

Contempt—The word contempt means to despise, which means to regard as worthless or distasteful. This usually applies to how you feel about the person who has betrayed your trust along with the person or persons he is betraying you with whether it is another woman or a "Pornelope" in some video chat room. Contempt is a necessary ingredient in the enemy's recipe for unforgiveness.

If you've been paying attention as you read, you now know that not forgiving is a prayer answer blocker. While you are going to have to forgive the other person or people involved in your hard situation, I have yet to meet a woman who could do this on her own. God is always willing to assist you with this and once He does, you can then begin praying for their salvation, too. Don't bail out now; I promise you'll be able to do this one day soon.

Think about how your spouse has been deceived into believing that porn is okay. Think about how you were once deceived into thinking that it was all right with God for you to manipulate and guilt-trip your spouse so that he would change for the better. Think about how you have rationalized your anger, even your rage, and your accusations.

Now realize that these are the same ways the other woman or the model peddling the porn has been deceived by Satan into thinking that what they are doing is all right. When you look at it like that, you may even start to feel pity for her or them. The contempt or disgust you have felt for the fact that they earn their living as family-wrecking balls will gradually dissolve into pity, perhaps even compassion, for how they are believing the enemy's lies. Prayer works for them, too (remember praying with the ripple effect).

From God

Hope—Also known as "the butterflies." This is that tickle you get in your belly out of the blue and you just know the whole thing is going to work out. I believe this is God's way of giving you a good look at His plan for success. Hope comes only from above. Hang on to it because God never gives us His hope for the impossible. Romans 5:5 says that hope in God does not disappoint us!

From The Enemy

Doubt—This is Satan's favorite day killer. One minute you're at the top of the world and full of hope; the next thing you know, he crashes your party with a thought like "This situation has gone too far to be fixed; there is too much water under the bridge." More people than I care to mention have given up on God simply because they fell for the devil's lies and doubt game.

But what if God is saying no? When God says no and you are in line with His will, walking with Him the way you are supposed to, it rarely hurts if you need to turn in another direction. Left turns, right turns, and even U-turns will be mostly painless when your heart is lined up with His. You will feel His peace, which assures you that you are going the right way.

This doesn't mean you won't have days when you are unable to hold on to His peace, and you find yourself getting tossed around on a rough sea. But when the peace returns and envelops you, you will know you're going in the right direction. Doubt is simply a lack of confidence in the promises He has given you. If there is one thing we can and should count on, it's that we can have confidence in God! He will never fail us!

Go back to His Book and read His promises; then place your confidence in the fact that He cannot lie. Let that restore your hope.

From God

Joy—The joy you feel is from above, a feeling like sunshine bursting out of your heart. The longer you stick to this journey, the more you will feel it. I like to believe that joy is God smiling down on us. Joy is His way of communicating that He is proud of how far we have come and how well we are doing. Joy is when you feel content when the circumstances around you look hopeless because you know you have God and nothing is too big for Him!

From The Enemy

Jealousy—This is a wicked human emotion that has absolutely no good in it at all. It is a lot of evil things wrapped into one feeling that has been responsible for everything from divorce to murder throughout time. The only one who has the right to be jealous is God, for His jealousy over you and me is a holy jealousy. It is a jealousy born out of His desire to have our love and adoration because He loves us so much. He wants and deserves for us to worship no other god but Him. He does not want us worshipping idols such as money, men, women, kids, material things, etc.

God is the only One who can righteously handle the power of jealousy.

When the enemy slides jealousy into your situation, things can really spin out of control. Usually, a situation isn't nearly as bad as jealousy portrays it, but jealousy is a wounding of the pride that causes even the nicest of people to do the most unspeakable things. Nothing feels worse or invokes jealousy more than knowing that your spouse is telling another woman the things he used to tell you and should still be telling you—things that should be reserved for only the two of you. Knowing this leaves you feeling worthless and wondering what the recipient of his affection has that you don't.

The devil has a powerful arrow with jealousy, and actions based on this emotion can be irreversible. It is the best tool he has for bringing out his reflection in us. Whether you are feeling a little jealous or violently jealous, you must take immediate steps to overcome the feeling. Start with prayer and even consider talking to a spiritual leader or whoever he or she recommends.

If you are feeling jealous, do not do anything you know you will regret later. If you're feeling like acting on the jealous urges, stop and look ahead to the possible outcome of your actions. Even though you are praying and trying your best to walk with the Lord, you are still responsible for your actions and the consequences.

One of the key components of jealousy is insecurity. Granted, you have your reasons to feel insecure right now. But try to focus on the positive things about yourself and your God, and this will help you deal with the situation a little better. You have to understand and believe that your spouse being addicted to pornography doesn't mean that there is something wrong with you. This is his problem, not yours.

Every time you feel jealous over whom he may be speaking to or what he may be doing, you have to tell yourself that he is being deceived. The thing that is enticing him is merely an illusion of a fantasy he has; it isn't a real situation. It is only happening because your spouse is paying for it to happen. The person on the other end is not some gorgeous and wonderful woman who is better than you; the person on the other end is a pornography model who has sold herself for a membership fee.

Not only that, think of it this way: You are in a full-scale battle for the restoration and preservation of your family. The best way for the enemy to take your focus off that victory is to overwhelm you with destructive details that you have no control over. You probably already know that you will always make the worst choices and biggest mistakes when you are angry. Jealousy's main component is anger.

See this feeling for what it is—a trick from the devil to set you back and cause you to take actions that will cost you this victory. Don't give him the satisfaction!

From God

Trust—After I came to know the Lord and had learned to trust Him, it always amazed me how humans will trust each other instead of trusting the One who both created them and wants to bless them. People will actually continue to place their trust in friends, family, and spouses even after they have failed them time and again.

The Lord is incapable of failing you. Don't give up on Him before He can complete the pieces of your picture, and then call it failure. There is a guaranteed good result in every situation He has allowed in your life if you cooperate with Him and let Him be God. The only thing you have to do is trust Him! Trust is assured reliance on the character, ability, strength, or truth of someone or something. This is a no-brainer.

The character of all humans is sinful. Our ability is limited, we are weak when we need to be strong, and integrity or truth can be hit or miss with us. So why do we place our trust for important answers in other humans instead of in God who has a perfect, upright character and the ability to do anything? We are our own worst enemy, aren't we?

The most common response I read on a daily basis in hundreds of letters is, "I can't *see* God. It's hard for me to trust Him when I can't see Him." You can't see air, but you know it's there and you trust that it will sustain your life. You can't see your heart, but you know it's there, and you trust that it is pumping life through you.

God directs us in the Bible to "*be anxious for nothing, but in everything by prayer and supplication, with thanksgiving, let your requests be made known to God...*" (Philippians 4:6, NKJV). He then adds the promise of things to come when we follow this directive, "*... and the peace of God, which surpasses all understanding, will guard your hearts and minds through Christ Jesus*" (Philippians 4:7, NKJV).

In other words, He's saying that you should not worry about your problem. You should humbly request what you will from Him in a serious and focused state of mind, and He will let His peace wrap around your heart and protect your mind through your faith in Jesus. Trusting God boils down to whether or not we believe what He says is true.

Do NOT confuse obedience for trust. It is much easier to be obedient to God's commands than it is to trust Him to do what He has said He would do. Trust has to be based on a true belief that He exists and that He is capable of doing what you have asked Him to do. Once you truly and sincerely trust in God, it is all downhill from there.

From The Enemy

Rebellion—This is a really ugly tool in the enemy's arsenal. We all go through it; some of us even mix pride in with it which really makes matters worse. Rebellion is a guaranteed miracle-delayer, if you ask me.

If you feel like you know more than God about what should happen, if you openly oppose His methods for bringing your problems to a good conclusion, and if you think that He could have done things in a much better way without the pain you've felt, you ARE a rebel. When you think you can do a better job than God, you're mimicking Satan's behavior. He thought he knew better than God, too.

I had a friend who had been a Christian for most of her life, but then she backslid over career reasons. She had spent over thirty years of her life totally dedicated to her work. She had been married several times, but the marriages ended because she was a workaholic. She had one child who lived in another state. Aside from the fact that she was a workaholic, she was a good person, she had more integrity than most people, and nearly everyone who knew her liked her. She was always focused on getting the job done the best way possible.

My friend had worked her way up the corporate ladder almost to the top when she found herself in the middle of a situation where she felt there was no way out of except to resign. She had gone on so long doing things her way and on her terms that allowing God into the driver's seat of this situation never even entered her mind. So she resigned.

After two years of depression and the lack of needed confidence to step back into her game, she became bitter and angry. She blamed God for all her problems. I reminded her that God doesn't make mistakes; we do. Her response was that God had gone too far. He had overshot the point this time. Maybe in her eyes He did; but while she was fussing and feeling sorry for herself, God was going right ahead changing her situation without her even noticing it.

She was isolated from her friends at work, she felt no one would hire her again in her field, and she now believed her education and experience were useless. Then she began to believe that everyone was turning against her. As she felt like she was losing control and falling apart, I began gently guiding her and telling her that she had nothing to lose by trusting in God for a good outcome. Actually what I told her was, "You have nothing to lose and everything to gain!"

Within a few months she was so broken she began to pray. As she did, doors started opening. She was offered a job in a field similar to the one she had been in, and although it felt like a step down, I convinced her to believe that God often closes one door so He can open another one. I urged her to see that this might be a door of opportunity that she wouldn't have been willing to look at while she was going her own way without His guidance.

She still insisted that God didn't have to go to such great lengths to get her attention. I assured her that if He had gone to such great lengths, it must have been necessary. We moved forward in her coaching one step at a time, and within a year she was promoted to supervisor in the company she had begun working for. Then she was offered another supervisor position in another company. But God had another plan.

One day out of the blue while she was surfing the Net she came across a company similar to the one she had resigned from. It was in the same field but at entry level, and she would have to go through a half year of training before she became eligible to advance.

She felt her history would prevent her from getting the job, but she sent the head of the company an e-mail that was surely dictated by the Lord Himself. She humbled herself and told the manager of her past situation. Within days she had interviewed, she had passed all of the required tests to work for this company, and she was hired. She was back in the game!

She was also a very changed person after the journey she had taken; she was a person who didn't want to make a move without praying about it. As a result, she was promoted through the ranks faster than anyone!

God didn't just change her geography; He changed her heart and her attitudes. She is now married to a wonderful Christian man and they are both faithful church members who are actively involved in the Church and their community. You wouldn't believe the person she has become. She is making a difference in peoples' lives with her testimony, and she is a great encourager for people who think their lives are over. God didn't overshoot the point; He repositioned her so she finally got His point! He blessed her with ten times more than she had before.

She might have started off stubborn and prideful, but the Lord cleansed her of those things. As He did, she allowed herself to accept His best for her even though it looked futile in the beginning. She quit rebelling against what God wanted to bless her with, and she was blessed many times over. Rebellion is a miracle blocker!

Rule number one: God knows everything and He knows it better than any human on earth. Rule number two: The longer you continue to play "know it all" or "know it better," the longer it is going to take for Him to create the heart He is trying to create in you. This in turn means that you have to wait for your miracle a lot longer than you need to. Trust me, I know.

I remember one point in my walk when I was so frustrated with the way God was doing things. He was so slow! Didn't He know how much I hated to have to wait? I threw a monumental Italian temper tantrum and threatened to give up. I even threw my Bible out the window. As if I was the only one in the world who mattered in His master plan! What a jerk I was. It took me four hours, during which time God was waiting patiently for me to get over it, to go out and retrieve my Bible and beg for forgiveness that I really didn't deserve.

Rebellion will get you nowhere! The devil likes that because the longer you wait without God's peace and with no sign of anything happening (to your eyes at least), the easier it is for him to take those shots that bring you closer to giving up.

From God

Hunger for His Word—When the longing to know more about Him starts moving you to read the Bible and you can't seem to get enough, you are longing to be in His presence. What better way to have a relationship than to get a fuller knowledge of the One you are having the relationship with! Unlike your human relationships, you will never be disappointed in what you find out about God. You will only find that He really is perfect.

As you read the Scriptures, the history of His world is intriguing. To think, the One who created the universe, all the animals, and everything else on earth, the One who whispered the victory plan into the ears and hearts of the prophets and warriors centuries ago, is the same One who is guiding you in your life today!

It doesn't get any better than that. Now, you need to let this sink into every fiber of your being and really believe it. Then let the power of such a revelation guide you!

From The Enemy

Depression—This is one of those weapons that you don't always recognize. You will often pass off the signs of depression as stress or fatigue from having so many things going on at once. If you've been feeling some combination of the following symptoms, you should see your Spiritual Doctor and a medical doctor as soon as possible.

Emotional

- Sadness throughout the day, nearly every day
- Loss of interest in or enjoyment of your favorite activities
- Feelings of emptiness or hopelessness
- Feeling stressed, nervous, or overwhelmed
- Trouble concentrating or making decisions
- Feelings of worthlessness
- Excessive or inappropriate feelings of guilt
- Irritability or restlessness
- Thoughts of death or suicide

Physical

- Fatigue or lack of energy
- Sleeping too much or too little
- Change in appetite or weight
- Aches and pains
- Headache
- Back pain
- Digestive problems
- Dizziness

Anytime you've experienced a major life upheaval (a spouse's porno addiction certainly qualifies here!), depression is often a result. Some people believe that they don't need a human doctor when they have put their faith in the Great Healer. I am not questioning God's ability to heal anyone of anything, but I do believe that He has given some people—doctors for instance—the knowledge and wisdom to administer treatment that helps heal us. Their help, combined with your faith and God's faithfulness, can bring you through this dangerous affliction with flying colors.

It's tough, darn near impossible in fact, to function normally let alone wage a full-scale spiritual war when you are dealing with the symptoms of depression. Please, don't hesitate. Go and get help today.

From God

Faith—This is an unshakable belief, trust, and loyalty in His ability to restore, repair, and replenish life, your marriage, or your situation coupled together with a firm belief that He wants to and He will. It has been said that the Book of Hebrews is the biblical account of faith. It's a wonderful place to go when you need a boost in your faith. When we have faith in God's Word, His promises come to life for us. They make this journey easier without a doubt.

From The Enemy

Separated From God—Are you feeling like God is a million miles away and He might never come back again? Perhaps you feel like your prayers are bouncing off the ceiling right back at you. You feel separated from God. There is only one thing that separates any of us from God: sin.

The devil will lead you astray as often as he can or as often as you let him. God will always forgive you and take you back. Remember that when Satan is telling you you've gone too far and that God won't take you back this time. Don't let anything, not a mistake or a bad day or even a bad decision, keep you from the love of God or take you where the grace of God can't protect you. No matter what, unload your spiritual baggage each day and fall into His loving arms.

From God

Patience—Plain and simple, patience is the ability to wait on your miracle without complaining or worrying while absorbing everything God is teaching you. A little advice: don't pray for patience. Trust me. Just BE patient. Ask anyone who has done this and they will tell you the same thing.

From The Enemy

Despair and Restlessness—Restlessness is an uneasy, discontented, unsettled feeling. You aren't really sure if you're coming or going. You can't stabilize your emotions and you can't feel peace. It's an ugly feeling that you get in the pit of your stomach. It causes frustration and even impatience with God. It's the enemy's way of stirring the pot and provoking you to do something that will separate you from the Lord.

Despair is basically all the things from Satan wrapped into one big ball. When he finds a way to drop it on you, it leaves you feeling devastated and hopeless. Sometimes the devil will find a weakness in your life and use it as a back door to make you feel despair. As your faith grows, you will learn to recognize his tricks sooner and sooner. Always be alert and aware that he keeps trying to find new ways to penetrate your faith.

Don't let that discourage you. His efforts to get at you can be used to learn more and more about how to reject his methods of dragging God's people down. The more you learn, the more you can help others realize how to avoid Satan's tactics as well.

From God

Delight—Now here is a gift from above that holds much promise. One of the greatest promises in the Bible is found in Psalm 37:4, *"Delight yourself in the* LORD *and he will give you the desires of your heart"* (NIV). In this Scripture God directs you to *delight* in Him, and He will give you the desires of your heart. WOW! That is awesome.

So how does one delight in God? When you delight in God, basically you are extremely satisfied with Him and all He is doing for you. The knowledge that He is present and directly involved in all aspects of your life and not just the problem that brought you to Him should bring you great joy. Once you sincerely delight in Him, He has promised to give you the desires of your heart! Actually, He's the One who puts those desires there.

Now that you have a general idea of what comes from where, you can better identify why you are feeling what you are feeling, and you have a better idea about how to deal with those feelings. This helps you travel through your journey a little easier. Keep this section handy and refer back to it whenever you need to. After awhile, the gift of discernment (which God gives us) will start to peek through any confusion you might have and you will know in your heart what is of God and what is not.

Your Spiritual Armor

Evil (or the enemy) is a very real force you have to reckon with. His sole purpose on earth is to deceive as many people as he can so they can share the same fate he is destined to. God gives you every lifeline you need to be sure that doesn't happen to you; you need only choose to grab them. He also gives you the spiritual armor that is necessary for this spiritual battle. He knew that once you invited Him into your life, the battle for your soul would rapidly begin.

If you aren't familiar with this spiritual armor, let me tell you about it. Read about it, go out on your own and find more about it; then let it penetrate your heart and mind. It is a very important part not only of this journey, but your lifelong journey with God. Learning about and understanding the importance of Ephesians 6:11-18 is vital to every Christian. To a new Christian, these verses will give an insight into what's going on behind the scenes.

Ephesians 6:13-18 tells us this: *"Put on the full armor of God so that you can take your stand against the devil's schemes. For our struggle is not against flesh and blood, but against the rulers, against the authorities, against the powers of this dark world and against the spiritual forces of evil in the heavenly realms. Therefore put on the full armor of God, so that when the day of evil comes, you may be able to stand your ground, and after you have done everything, to stand. Stand firm then, with the belt of truth buckled around your waist, with the breastplate of righteousness in place, and with your feet fitted with the readiness that comes from the gospel of peace. In addition to all this, take up the shield of faith, with which you can extinguish all the flaming arrows of the evil one. Take the helmet of salvation and the sword of the Spirit, which is the word of God. And pray in the Spirit on all occasions with all kinds of prayers and requests. With this in mind, be alert and always keep on praying for all the saints"* (NIV).

Let's break this down so you can utilize it in your everyday walk.

1. The belt of truth represents Jesus Christ and the Gospel, thus the importance of reading and literally absorbing the Bible. His Word is the truth and knowing that the truth will always set you free!

2. The breastplate of righteousness is living according to the truth and walking in His ways. To be righteous means acting in accord with divine or moral Law or being free from guilt or sin. The best way to understand this is that you cannot be righteous if you are living in sin. You can't be protected from the fiery darts of the evil one if you are being unrighteous.

3. Feet fit with readiness to share the Gospel of peace is like wearing special shoes that are obtained from faith in His Word. The whole core or center of the Gospel of peace is the message of salvation that comes through the cross of Christ. The Gospel reconciles people who were previously separated from Him to Him. It also reconciles people who are or have been hostile toward one another (Ephesians 2:14-16). This would explain the paradox of why the Gospel of peace has often been used in the arena of holy wars.

4. The shield of faith is fully trusting God and His ability to help you reject all doubts planted by the devil and all of his fiery darts.

5. The helmet of salvation is used to protect your head, or in this case your thoughts. It represents something Christ is doing in you and, even more importantly, through you in this world. The helmet of salvation works to keep your thinking straight. It preserves you from mental confusion and darkness also known as despair.

6. The Sword of the Spirit is the Word of God. It is the authority of Scripture. Knowing His Word helps you to have more power and authority over evil than you can imagine, and as you travel along you will come to know more and more how to use this power.

Through his intelligence, Satan deceived Adam and Eve and took over their rule of the world for himself (Genesis 1:26; 3:1-7; 2 Corinthians 11:3). His cleverness enables him to carry out his deceptive work almost at will, but his power is subject to God's restrictions. The reins of God on his activities are illustrated by Satan's request to God for permission to afflict Job (Job 1:7-12). The devil's influence in worldly affairs is also clearly revealed in John 12:31.

Satan's nature is malicious. His efforts in opposing God, His people, and His truth are tireless. He is always opposed to man's best interests. Through his role in introducing sin into the human family (Genesis 3), Satan gained the power of death—a power which Christ broke through His crucifixion and resurrection.

Satan is permitted to afflict God's people, but he is never permitted to win an ultimate victory over them. He isn't a winner; he's a loser. You are not a victim of his lies. You have to choose to believe the lies. So, just choose not to make that choice! Hopefully your trip will be a little more stable and rooted in His promises and truth as you are armed with this information.

12

Going about God's Business While He Goes about Yours

Divine Education

Who could have known that pornography was going to invade your life? How could you have been ready for it? Unfortunately, pornography strikes families like a bolt of lightning out of nowhere. All you know is that all at once everyone's life is turned upside down. It is literally impossible to carry on the way you did before such a storm hits. You're crazy if you think life can go on the same way it did before by pretending hard enough that nothing has happened.

There is an old adage I like to use when I teach, "The definition of insanity is to keep doing the same thing over and over and expect different results each time." A lot of us learn this the hard way, but I am hoping you will take the crash course and move beyond this blessing blocker.

With each lesson you learn, there has to be the foundation of divine wisdom. The Lord says that if you ask Him, He will give you wisdom. *"Call to me and I will answer you and show you great and mighty things, fenced in and hidden, which you do not know"* (Jeremiah 33:3).

As you grow closer to the Lord, the power I keep telling you about that is contained in the Scriptures, His living Word, will come alive to you. Although you don't understand everything all at once, God reveals all that you do need to know at the perfect time in your walk. He'll arm you with the wisdom you need to make the right decisions and take the right actions at the right time. You'll just have to choose to do it.

As a Christian I believe that every word in the Bible was given from God to the holy men of God who wrote it (2 Peter 1:21). Today's skeptic might say that the Bible is simply a bunch of writing written by men who put their own interpretations and spin put upon it. No, IT'S NOT! That's what the enemy wants you to think to make it easier for you to try to lower the standards of the Bible to the world's standards instead of raising yours to those of the Bible. If you choose to believe this lie, you'll find that the power the Word of God contains will never be revealed to you because you because you will have blocked it with your unbelief.

Many people say the Bible was written a long, long time ago and that the things that were done back in "biblical days" aren't relevant anymore. How wrong these unbelievers are. That is just an excuse to live outside the rules set forth within it. The Bible is a perfect road map for our lives. It always has been.

Although we have changed our dress code a bit and our technology is far greater, the principles of God's Word are still and will always stay the same until the end of time. God asks that you do things a certain way, and then He promises you something in return. The rewards you will receive are mostly spiritual and far more valuable than any material item.

For instance, if you had to place a value on the one you love, the one you are fighting for right now, how much would you pay for him to be completely free and whole? How much would you pay to have his undying love and respect for the rest of your life? Wouldn't you be willing to pay more for that than you would for a chain of luxury hotels, two huge mansions, three yachts, and a garage full of fancy sports cars? I was once in a position where I was holding a pile of money and a broken heart, and I would have paid any amount and given anything I had to have my love returned.

In the beginning of our journey with God, we all approached Him with a "gimme" and in some cases, "Gimme, please!" Our relationship with Him was completely one-sided at that point, and we were totally ignorant of the promises He had for us and the things we needed to do to obtain those promises. As I said earlier, you can't build a good relationship with catchers' mitts on both of your hands. It's no different with God.

You must decide if you really want to know Him or if you just want His blessings and help when you think you need them. If you honestly want to know Him, then it is only through reading His Word and meditating upon it that you can truly find out who He really is and how much He loves you. The Bible reveals sides of His character that you have never really known existed. As you learn more about His character, you will deeply and genuinely fall in love with Him.

This will be like the love you have perhaps felt for someone, love that was so strong that the thought of this person not being in your life could cause you great pain and sorrow. This is the kind of love you'll feel when you fall in love with Him, only it will be much stronger than the strongest emotion you have ever felt so far.

Understanding God's Side of Your Relationship

I believe that God has a reason and a purpose for everything He does. He doesn't just single people out to torture them or put them through testing and trials to see what they can take. He knows you right down to the very core of your soul better than you know yourself. This is exactly why there are times when He will not give you what you are asking for.

He knows if what you are asking for is good or bad for you and if it will cause you great pain or even harm at some point. You are unable to see that far ahead into your life;

you only know that something seems to be missing and you want whatever you believe will fix it.

Throughout His Word He reveals to you the reasons He does what He does. Most new believers I talk to almost always ask, "Does God expect me to be a mind reader? How can I know what His will for my life is if He won't show me?" He does show us. Throughout His book, He reveals His will and gives us a blueprint for life. As we draw closer to Him, He reveals more and more.

So we start off with our "gimme" in our hands and we approach the throne of God totally desperate for relief. When we don't receive an instant answer from Him, we often turn back to trying to manipulate things to go our way for a while. Finally, however, most of us reach the point where we look up and say "Okay, Lord! What do you want me to do now?"

Do you ever wonder if God says, *"Just open up your Bible and start reading. All of my answers and instructions are right there"*?

More About Delighting Yourself in the Lord

One day as I was reading the Bible, I came across one of my now favorite Scriptures: Psalm 37:4, *"Delight in the Lord and He will give you the desires of your heart."* "Wooo Hooo!" I yelled, "I found the key! Finally!" I closed the Bible, went and sat by the phone, and waited for it to ring. I knew that when it did, my miracle would be on the other end.

I waited … and I waited. Then it rang. It was a recorded message telling me my library books were past due. I figured maybe the library accidentally got through to my phone first, so I waited some more. Back then, you can see that I didn't have much of a life. The high point of my day was when the library's auto-attendant called to remind me to bring my books back. Hey, at least someone thought to call me. When the call I was waiting for didn't come, I got angry.

I looked up at the ceiling and said aloud, "God! You said ALL I had to do was delight in you! I just don't understand!" I cried. "I've been praying and waiting and reading and waiting and waiting and waiting!"

This was definitely not delight.

"I can't figure out what You want from me, and I am so tired of all of this waiting. You're GOD! You can do anything! So why don't You?" I was pitching a monumental hissy fit in the middle of my laundry room over my belief that God really didn't know what He was doing up there.

This was really not delight.

After I calmed down and realized what a jerk I was, I felt the Lord surround me with peace. He had shown me that promise for a reason. He reminded me of our covenant made on the beach the day that I said, "I will learn all You have to teach me if You will just fix my heart."

Okay, so what more was there to learn? I had been waiting THREE whole months, and I had absorbed everything I thought I possibly could. Wrong, I hadn't learned how to delight in Him. When I swallowed enough of my pride, I asked God to show me how to delight in Him so that I could be in line with that promise. He had given me a directive: Delight in Him according to His standards, and He would honor His promise to give me the desires of my heart.

Two things happened in that lesson. First, I learned that delight was much more than praying and asking and reading for my personal gain. Delight was being happy with just God in my life. It was being content with Him even if it meant Shaun would never come back. This tied in with God's promise that "His grace was sufficient."

The second thing I learned was that what I thought was all I needed was for Shaun to come back was not my true desire. God knew, being far more able to see the true desires of my heart than I could, that my real desire was for love from someone who would return that love on the same level. The answer that I finally got was indeed perfect. It was what my heart really wanted and needed—not what my mind thought I needed.

When we educate ourselves about Him first and foremost and then begin to practice His ways, we prepare ourselves for the wisdom He will bless us with. Many times, deep into our walk with Him, we can be talking to someone and say something particularly insightful. Then later, we look back on it and say, "Where did that come from?" It came from Above. It was His wisdom.

Going about God's Business while He Goes about Yours

Every one of us has taken on more than we can handle at one time or another. Right now you are probably way overloaded. You may be dealing with a job, a family, a household, kids' activities, shopping, bill-paying, laundry day, extended family, and all that these things entail, like soccer games and family functions. To top it all off, you have a marriage that feels like it is on the rocks right now.

That's an awfully big load to try to carry on your own. In addition to that you are trying to learn all God has to teach you without making any more mistakes in the middle of a situation that you really haven't had any prior experience with. That's a mouthful, isn't it?

There is relief in sight if you're ready to surrender some of the load. You may have tried everything you could think of to "fix" the porn problem, and by now you should be realizing that you cannot fix it. At least not alone. You can contribute to the repairs, but fixing it is out of your hands even if you are a clone of Wonder Woman.

You've made some good decisions up to this point and the first one was calling the Lord into the situation. The bad part may be that you called Him in, but you're still trying to fix the problem. In order for Him to fix it, you have to let go of it. Easier said than done, I know. There is a poem I once read about letting go:

Let Go and Let God

As children bring their broken toys
With tears for us to mend,
I brought my broken dreams to God
Because He is my friend.

But then, instead of leaving Him
In peace to work alone;
I hung around and tried to help,
With ways that were my own.

At last, I snatched them back and cried,
"How could You be so slow?"
"My child," He said. "What could I do?
You never did let go."
Author: Lauretta P. Burns

That little poem really describes the way things happen when we bring a broken dream to God. We pray and try to draw close to Him, hanging onto His robes with one hand; but the whole while our other hand is hanging on to the problem. One hand on Him, one hand on the problem. Nothing can get fixed that way: not us; not the problem.

A staggering number of people come to my website determined to let God take care of things, but then they step back into the situation and try to fix it their own way. Not good, not good at all. Let me tell you about a friend of mine from *Just4Ladies* who fixed her situation beyond repair.

Donna came to *Just4Ladies* totally desperate for God to fix her broken relationship with her boyfriend Jake. They had been together for about a year, but Jake decided he just didn't want to be in such a serious relationship. Donna and Jake were both in their late twenties and Donna was ready to settle down. Jake was her ninth or tenth serious boyfriend, but she was *really* sure Jake was *the one* now.

The day Jake broke things off with Donna, she thought she would die. Instead of letting him go off to think about the situation, she made a scene in a public parking lot by crying hysterically and insisting she wouldn't let him go. She even attempted to block him when he went to get into his car. Not a good way to convince someone that you're the girl of his dreams!

Jake got away and for the next two weeks he refused to take Donna's calls. One time he accidentally picked up his work phone and it was her, crying. He told her that her behavior had confirmed for him that he wasn't ready to be that serious. He told her he was surprised at how she was acting and that he had seriously thought about getting back to her until she started calling him twenty times a day.

Donna was fixing it beyond repair.

When Jake succeeded in avoiding her altogether on the phone, Donna began e-mailing him. She begged and pleaded and groveled. She told him how miserable she was without him in hopes that he would feel sorry for her. When that didn't work, she told him she was going to kill herself. That didn't work, either. She was expecting Jake to run to her side to try to stop her and when she didn't get the reaction she wanted, she e-mailed him again with hateful words.

This was a classic example of "Action for Reaction," and as in almost all cases, it failed and made things way worse. Finally, defeated and exhausted, Donna found *Just4Ladies. com*. She described the entire story to me in detail. Needless to say, Donna needed step-by-step coaching to force her to focus on herself and not Jake. Her entire days were filled with thoughts of Jake, how to get Jake to talk to her, what Jake was doing, who Jake was doing it with—Jake, Jake, Jake. This was not healthy at all!

So step-by-step we walked Donna toward the Lord, and little by little we helped her focus on herself, her attitude, and her actions. We did some reverse role playing where what she was doing to Jake was being done to her. She admitted that she didn't like it. About six months into our hard work, Jake called her. He hadn't heard from her in a while and was wondering if she was okay. His call was simply a courtesy to check on her welfare.

She did really well, and they ended up going out to dinner as friends. One thing led to another and Donna encouraged Jake to stay the night with her which he did.

After that weekend Donna began bombarding Jake with e-mails and phone calls again. She skipped out of all of the sessions with me, and figured God had answered her prayer because Jake was back in her life. But after a week of Jake avoiding her calls, she came back to *Just4Ladies* in the exact same condition she had several months earlier. None of the progress we had made was evident at all.

Once again we started to move forward, but Donna was still determined to get Jake back. She felt she could manipulate him back and once he was back, he would see how great they were together. Three weeks after their evening together, Donna e-mailed Jake and told him she was pregnant. She was lying.

Jake avoided her like the plague after that, so she went to his job to confront him. He told her he was involved with someone else and she could do whatever she decided to do about the "baby." He told her not to contact him anymore.

Donna had fixed it beyond repair.

Her ways were not better than God's ways and only resulted in her never having a chance with Jake again. Jake is now married to someone else. At one point during this situation Jake's heart had softened toward Donna. Was that God softening it? We'll never know. Instead of leaving her situation in God's hands and waiting peacefully while the Lord worked in her heart, which would have given her the ability to see and accept His will for her relationship with Jake, she instead took everything back into her own hands and totally destroyed it with her actions.

But how can God be God and not be able to fix something even if you've broken it? He can and He even will in many cases. But you have to stay out of His way and out of His dealings with your situation and the people who are in it with you. Remember the title of this chapter: Going about God's Business While He Goes about Yours? That means you work on learning more about Him, understanding His way, and surrendering to Him, and you let Him be God over everything else.

Twenty-One Days of Change

So how do you do that? The first time you try something is always the most intimidating. They say it takes twenty-one days to form a new habit or break an old one. This is one of the theories I use in teaching, and it has produced impressive results for the people who have utilized it. So let's get started.

The first step is to be aware of when you are trying to control the situation. For example, your spouse is headed to the study and you know what he is going to do when he gets online. Instead of picking a fight with him, which will undoubtedly push him further into wanting the escape he feels when he's online, try saying nothing. I really mean say nothing, no body language that shows your disgust, no dirty looks, nothing.

Close your eyes and say, "Lord, I know what he is going to do and nothing I say or do is going to stop him from doing it. Only You can handle this situation." For twenty-one days, choose to literally surrender to God whatever your husband is doing to feed his addiction. It may seem really hard, but this is how you surrender control to the Lord. After you have done this, then force yourself to trust God to be working on the situation.

In the meantime, you focus on God and go about His business. Get your Bible out and start reading it. Go online and visit a prayer board (see recommendations at the back of the book) and pick out several prayers. Send someone who is having a difficult time a letter of encouragement. Do something good. Do something to fuel your spiritual fire. Add to the Lord's arsenal of spiritual weapons in your heart.

Instead of focusing on what your spouse may or may not be doing, focus your thoughts on the end result of knowing God better and letting Him handle your business. Daydream about the day when everything will be good again. No, focus on what it will be like when everything is better than it ever was before. When God is involved and at the helm, you won't get just good; you will get great!

Don't fall victim to the "what if's":

- What if he falls in love with one of these bimbos?
- What if he takes my lack of reaction as approval for what he is doing?
- What if God doesn't want to fix this?
- What if he spends so much money on porn that we can't pay our bills?
- What if the sky falls tomorrow or a plane crashes into our home?

Almost none of the "what if's" ever happen when we are on guard and God is in control. When you let Him be in control, He won't let anything happen that He can't handle. Remember that when you start to panic.

Things may look like they are going in the complete opposite direction of a good result, but the fact of the matter is that you have given the situation to God and it's His responsibility now. So, don't try to take it back! God may have to allow certain things to happen that look like the world coming to an end through your eyes, but in reality He is using the situation to change the one you are praying for.

When you surrender totally to God, there is nothing that is broken that He cannot fix so long as you leave it with Him. There is nothing that has been done or is being done that He cannot undo. I am talking about everything from finances to your spouse leaving altogether. If you are truly letting God be in control of your situation, the end result is guaranteed to be for your good (Romans 8:28). It's really quite simple once you let the facts sink in.

• You have a situation that looks impossible. *God does the impossible. Nothing is impossible for Him. Nothing.*

• You have tried everything you know to remedy the situation and it only seems to get worse. *Take the pressure off yourself and trust God enough to give it all to Him.*

• You gave everything you knew to give to God, but it's getting worse. *Trust that God has the solution and* LEAVE *it with Him! His ways are way higher than your ways. He parted the Red Sea, didn't He?*

Going about His business while He goes about yours guarantees that when He has restored what you have lost, you will be able to nurture it and not use the past to destroy it again. So even though you may think you are not the one who has to change, you will change, too.

The Only Way to Change Them is to Change You!

Most women feel that they are the innocent victims of their spouse's pornography addiction. If you're focused on thinking that you're the innocent one being hurt here, it's time to get out your suitcase again. You remember the one you were carrying all that old "stuff" in when you started this journey way back on page one?

You've come a long way, and you are doing a great job, and this should help you relax and love God even more: He'll keep right on loving you even if you aren't doing such a great job. His love is not based upon your performance as a perfect Christian; His full and faithful love is right there even when you blow it. He knows you're trying as hard to be where He wants you to be in the way He wants you to be there.

Important point, however! Even though He will still love you, His dealings with you and His help for you will change dramatically if you set yourself to fight against Him and rebel.

If your circumstances seem to be getting worse, that doesn't mean God has forsaken your situation. That is God is taking things completely apart before He puts them all back together. In some cases He lets things die spiritually so He can breathe new life into them. At this point, you may be experiencing that yourself.

You may have approached the cross feeling half-dead and fully defeated, but God has picked you up, brushed you off, given you a good cleansing, and redressed you in white garments that signify you are now part of His family. He has begun walking through your life with you whether you stumble or not. His outpouring of blessings and His help might be hindered if you keep insisting upon continuing to make wrong choices, but His presence and His love toward you will never change.

Did you stop loving your toddler when you cleaned her all up and dressed her all up and then she threw up all over it? Of course not, you loved her and cleaned her up again and dressed her up again. So, how many times will God be willing to do that? As many times as it takes. He's in this with you for the long haul, and that's not the human outlook on a long haul. He's in it with you for eternity!

Without knowing it, you have already done a lot of changing. If that makes you feel indignant and saying, "Why do I have to change? I didn't do anything wrong!" you can be certain that you still need to change some more. But why? Because if you stay in the same place with the same attitudes while your spouse changes, then things will really be difficult. Change in both people is necessary for a successful outcome.

Know that God is going about the business of softening your spouse's heart and bringing to the surface all the hurt he's caused everyone. Hold on to that when you don't think you can stand it another minute. Let God do what He needs to do.

I have met so many wives who have gotten their miracles, whose men have come back to reality, and are fully prepared to make a new start. But the wives just didn't have the strength it took to leave their "whys" alone. The second you open that Pandora's Box, you're asking for trouble. Men can only handle so much of you adding to the guilt they are already feeling. Bringing up your "whys" will do nothing productive; they will only initiate a guilt trip that will invariably turn ugly.

Don't Go Backwards

If you are making headway in your relationship recovery and you feel the overwhelming urge for confrontation regarding why your husband did what he did, you need to go back to the forgiveness step before you find yourself all the way back at step one wondering if you have the strength to start completely over again! Try hard to emulate the same forgiveness with others that God gives us: forgive and wipe the slate clean never to be revisited again. Nothing good can come from revisiting this situation once it is being overcome. Nothing at all. This is one big reason that a change in you is necessary in order for this to work.

I had the opportunity to speak to Jim who was a former "porn addict." Jim kicked his habit several years ago when he was on the verge of losing his family. I asked Jim how his marriage was after he gave up pornography, and he said that for a very long time he was not sure his marriage was going to survive.

Jim's wife was a good Christian woman who leaned on the Lord to get her through the storm. But when Jim started responding to the prayers she had been sending up, she forgot to keep trusting God. Day after day they would start off fine, but the slightest change in Jim's routine like going to the store for a pack of cigarettes would set her off on a tangent that would last long into the night. "She would accuse me of going back on my promises and wanting to leave the house so I could call other women."

Because he didn't discuss what he was feeling about his addiction with his wife, she instantly thought he was ignoring the fact that he had almost destroyed their marriage and family. Jim was holding himself accountable in his own way with the Lord and through prayer. But his wife couldn't surrender her hurt feelings and insecurities to God during this new phase of change, and she kept constantly throwing the whole situation in his face.

She had done this with many other things in the past that were not related to pornography, and it was simply a behavioral pattern for her. It took some pastoral counseling for Jim's wife to realize that she needed to change, too.

As each day comes to a close, you have to learn to put that day behind you because you can't go back and undo one thing; you can only deal with what you have in front of you. Each day is a new chance at living totally in the Lord. As you now know, His presence is the best place to be. Without Him, you find yourself doing everything in your own strength and not His. This makes it hard to hold on to the peace that has carried you this far and you'll find that you are setting yourself up for a setback.

Some days you'll get through like a champ. You won't be tempted to fight with your spouse over his addiction. You'll find that even with the gazillion responsibilities you have, you didn't carry anything that was too heavy or not meant for you to carry that day. When you give God the unfixable problems, the rest of your responsibilities are a breeze to deal with.

When you think differently, you will act differently. When you act differently, others around you will begin to change the way they act (including your spouse). Don't be hard on yourself if your attempts to change are sluggish. You've spent the last twenty, thirty, forty, or maybe more years getting used to the way you are. All of that isn't going to change overnight! Just celebrate the little changes when they come. Look for them so you don't miss them and then, it's Party Time!

Lasting, effective change is a gradual process. When it is done with God's guidance, it's easier because He reveals parts of you, bit by bit, that you need to change. Some things about you may be just fine, but because you have been thrust into a situation you were totally unprepared to deal with, those good features may be hidden by some of the bad ones you've been flailing about with.

Believe it or not, it is actually good when those things you need to change begin coming to the surface so you can recognize them and ask God to help you work on them. The only time it's bad is when you know that these things are there and you won't do anything about them. So, the order of the day is that it's out with the old and in with the new. Little by little this will happen as you let it.

Any mental health professional in the marriage therapy field will tell you that if you've come to him or her hoping for a way to change your spouse without changing yourself, give it up and go home.

Get a New Attitude!

Your attitude is what everything else ties back to. Once you have a change in attitude, the rest of the changing comes easier. So what exactly is attitude? *A complex mental state involving your beliefs and feelings and values and dispositions that cause you to act in certain ways* (WordNet). That sure does encompass every part of your psyche, doesn't it?

Self-justifying attitudes, wrong patterns of thought, and angry feelings can profoundly affect your mental state and your choices. Looking at Donna and Jake's story earlier, you can see how Donna's emotions caused her to go off the deep end.

If you find yourself crying at the drop of a dime, then maybe it's time to look deeper and find out what is causing you to feel so sensitive. Do not rule out a visit with your doctor or therapist. Sometimes when you are under extreme stress, your body produces less of the chemicals that your brain needs to function properly. This drop in body chemicals can affect sleep, appetite, alertness, and your capacity to feel pleasure and satisfaction.

Don't be ashamed to reach out to your medical professional for help. Although I want this book to help you, and I know that God will help you, it is a good idea to make sure that it isn't something medical that is hindering you from making great progress. Your doctor has been blessed with knowledge on how to help your body heal. Let him or her help you. A lot of the people I deal with express embarrassment at having to take medication to deal with something as emotional as this type of situation. Get out of that cycle and go see your doctor if you are finding it difficult just to get up and get through your days.

Another big component of positive change is your reaction factor. Your spouse is used to and even expects certain reactions from you in specific situations. As a result, he prepares himself for what he knows is probably coming. If your normal reaction to something negative he has done is an explosion and an all-out fight, this is a good time to look at how you can change that. Go to God in prayer and ask Him to help you.

If you react completely differently than you usually do, you'll so confuse your spouse that he won't know what to do with you. You will definitely have his attention!

If you determine right now, within the next ten seconds, to have a different attitude and a different reaction to everything (not just the porn addiction), you will begin to see a change in him! The secret to success with these changes is consistency. Consistency can seem to take the strength of an army because you might feel really fired up about this new concept today, and maybe you still will tomorrow. But after three or four episodes of demonstrating your changed attitude and reaction and you don't see any change in him, you may be tempted to just go back to your old ways. Don't do it.

Stay consistent and keep asking God for the grace and the strength to do so. Don't start running your old internal videos to show you why it is hopeless to try to move forward.

Note from Pastor Tom: Do you have inner conflicts? Do you know of anyone above the age of zero whose life is not filled with inner conflicts? Conflict is not really the problem, though. As a matter of fact, conflict can be good! As we work our way through the daily conflicts that dog our footsteps, with God's help we can find both our inner and outer strengths to solve problems. Then we can let these victory experiences help us learn how to solve even bigger problems.

Jesus knew that the way to deal with our conflicts was available, but that our old natures would fight going there. What we have to do is somehow assemble and focus all our energies, face in one direction, and move toward Him. Somehow, you have to discipline yourself to subdue and subordinate all your lesser loyalties to one Master loyalty. Jesus said, *"Seek ye first the kingdom of God and his righteousness, and all these things will be added unto you"* (Matthew 6:33).

There are three things we can do to resolve the pressures of inner conflict between our higher and lower natures. First, we *can* give in to the enemy believing that this will end the fight. Terrible consequences are around the corner from this one. Second, we *can* try to effect a compromise within the conflict. This is trying to "have it both ways," trying to carry the good and the evil at the same time. More bad consequences on the way. Third, we *could* (and SHOULD) just flat out surrender totally to God. Do that and you can be sure help is on the way!

We must be willing to bring our conflicts up to our Lord and face them. Otherwise we just submerge them more deeply in the unconscious or subconscious mind.

Then we must recognize our responsibility to change. We will set up all kinds of elaborate defenses to protect ourselves and to justify our feelings and our attitudes rather than face unpleasant facts which indicate that we might have some responsibility in our ongoing problems. Then we must decide what we will do about beginning to face the truth and build our lives upon the correct foundation.

At this point, we can begin to take full responsibility for our lives. We start porn-proofing our homes, we quit blaming the pornography industry for our situation, and we begin to refuse to buy and use the products of the "adult world." When we turn FROM SIN, we turn TO GOD.

Give yourself completely to the higher and the larger life in Christ, and your life will become unified, organized for action, happy, and satisfied.

Change takes daily effort. Start today with the twenty-one day method. Pick something you know you need to change and let today be day one in your effort. Keep track of your progress in a journal. You'll be amazed at how far you'll go in just twenty-one days.

13

Victory for Your Marriage Is Getting Nearer Every Day!

Don't Be Unequally Yoked with Unbelievers ... Even Old Friends

In addition to holding on to pride, resentment, guilt, anger, fear, pride, self-pity, jealousy, despair, pride, and selfishness, there are some other things you may need to turn away from as well. These are things from your past life that really don't fit in with your new beliefs and your new way of thinking; for instance, your unbelieving friends.

Do the people you call your friends believe the same things you do? Do you feel comfortable enough to share your newfound faith with them? Are you a bit afraid of what they will say if you do?

One woman I know gave up on her journey because her "friends" told her she was fighting a lost cause and she had become a "Bible thumper" because she went to church and had stopped going to the nightclubs on the weekends. In your new life, with friends like that you won't need enemies. The reason the Lord tells you to not be *unequally yoked* with unbelievers (2 Corinthians 6:16) is because unbelievers pull you away from Him and also away from your miracle.

The Bible does tell you that you are to be *salt* and *light* to the unbelieving world, so you cannot isolate yourself from others to do that. But you are not to become so "yoked" (tied to, controlled by) the world that unbelievers are in position to pull you away from your faith walk. You are in the world, but you are not to be of the world.

Picture a big glass of iced tea with its ice cubes clinking and condensation forming on the outside of the glass. You like your tea sweetened, so you add some sugar which goes right down to the bottom of the glass and just lies there. The sugar is IN the tea, but it is not PART OF the tea—not yet. As you stir the tea, the sugar begins to dissolve and becomes PART OF the tea. It has become OF the tea.

The Bible tells you that you are IN the world as witnesses to the truth, but you are not to be OF the world as you do so. You can do more research on this by reading 1 John 2:15; Romans 12:2; John 15:19; John 17:11,15,16; 2 Peter 1:4; and James 4:4.

Few things are harder than parting ways with longtime friends. If you have to admit to yourself that your friends do not really allow you to enjoy your faith when you are around them, then this may be a point where you have to decide what's more important—your friends or your faith. You do not need to cut them completely out of your life, but be careful of their attitudes toward your walk with God.

If you feel fairly comfortable being with them and they do not make fun or tease you about being a Christian, you may be able to continue to enjoy times with them. If you always feel a bit on guard around them, then ask yourself these questions:

• Do your friends encourage your faith even if they don't have it?

• Are they interested even a little bit in what you are finding out about your relationship with God?

• Do they make you feel uncomfortable to use the name of Jesus when you speak?

• Do they encourage you to bend your newfound principles just a tiny bit so that you can have some fun?

If they are not comfortable with your relationship with Him, your desire to spend time with these friends will probably taper off. You just won't have a lot of things in common with them anymore. You'll find yourself wanting to spend time with other believers because in doing so your faith is boosted, your knowledge is increased, and encouragement and hope is always just a hug or a kind godly word away.

Other things you may have to get rid of are worldly habits—things that don't seem terrible but that you know are not godly. In Pastor Tom's case, he had to give up chocolate cake. Let him tell you about his ex-best friend.

Note from Pastor Tom: I have a weight problem. It's not that I'm so much overweight; it's just that my bathroom scales lie about my weight. If I had a set of talking scales, I bet they would say, "One at a time, please." I've had to part with one of my former best friends over this—chocolate cake.

If I can't be best friends with a chocolate cake for obvious reasons, shouldn't the same thing be said about having "best" friends who would tempt you to adjust your walk with Christ (and not for the better)? It is not a sin to be tempted, but there comes a point where it is foolish to hang around if the temptations keep getting ratcheted up when you are around those friends.

The Bible says: "*Wherefore let him that thinks he stands take heed lest he fall. There hath no temptation taken you but such as is common to man: but God is faithful, who will not suffer you to be tempted above that ye are able; but will with the temptation also make a way to escape, that ye may be able to bear it. Wherefore, my dearly beloved, flee from idolatry*" (1 Corinthians 10:13-14).

Being tempted is not the problem; it is the yielding to temptation that is totally devastating. You need to realize how powerful sin is, and what Satan's agents of sin can and will do to keep you in their fold. You also need to realize how desperately they want to keep you from reading that there is an answer—a way out—a genuine solution to their hold over you!

There is real help available! The power of this help is waiting for every single one of God's children, from the meekest frustrated lamb to the great apostles of the Scriptures. In the Bible, one of my heroes is the apostle Peter. He had a few problems—actually a lot of his life was just one big problem after another. But he got his life on track, and Jesus used him in some powerful ways.

The apostle Paul was told to go see some guys that he didn't like who were doing stuff he didn't like, and he had a real problem with that. But after an object lesson from God in Acts 10, he set out to find these people with a clear message of hope and help. Here is what he decided: *"I perceive that the Lord is no respecter of persons"* (Acts 10:34). You can read what happened for yourself, but suffice it to say, the good guys won.

Just as God is no respecter of persons, the devil who is the tempter is likewise no respecter of persons. Believers should constantly be on guard against temptation. If they find that old friends make them feel tempted, then they may have to forsake them for the time being. The constant warning from Scripture is: "Take heed, flee." It is the same thing as that with which I started: "I can't be best friends with a chocolate cake I can't be trusted around." So I have to stay out of bakery shops, away from the dessert bar in restaurants, and other places where chocolate cakes lurk.

If I find myself with a chocolate cake right in front of me on the counter, it puts pressure on me every time I look at it. But if I don't have that cake around, the "sight and smell" temptation is not there and I am on my way to the right track. If we stay away from friends who try to pull us off our walk, we're on our way to winning. If we take the dirty pictures out of our homes, we're on our way to winning. If we block the suggestive channels on our televisions, we're on our way to winning.

The Lord neither tempts anyone to do wrong, nor has He ever promised anyone He would remove the temptation. What He does promise is grace to withstand it, and He knows that this is really all we need. Where did we ever get the crazy, mixed-up idea that we are in this thing alone? God knows what is going on in your life and what you are going through! He cares about every bit of it!

He knows how powerful and subtle that temptation from the devil is, and He stands right there beside you asking you to use all your strength in Him in resisting all temptations.

Leave it to a Baptist preacher to take the fun out of something as simple as a big piece of chocolate cake!

Make It Last Forever

The enemy knows you have grown spiritually stronger and that you are not as naïve to his tricks as you once were. Be prepared for him to find new ways to try to trick you. One of the most common things the enemy does at this stage of your faith is fill your head with worries about whether or not your spouse is the one God really wants for you.

He will even try to confuse God's own Word to make you fall for his tricks. A good example is the Scripture about being yoked with an unbeliever (2 Corinthians 6:14). Satan may try to convince you that now that you are a practicing member of God's own family and your spouse is not, you don't belong together.

This lie has brought many a woman who had been standing for her marriage to her knees feeling confused and questioning if what she had been hearing in her heart was truly God's guidance.

First Corinthians 7:12-14 tells you that the apostle Paul said this: *"To the rest I say this (I, not the Lord): If any brother has a wife who is not a believer and she is willing to live with him, he must not divorce her. And if a woman has a husband who is not a believer and he is willing to live with her, she must not divorce him. For the unbelieving husband has been sanctified through his wife, and the unbelieving wife has been sanctified through her believing husband. Otherwise your children would be unclean, but as it is, they are holy"* (NIV).

Verse 15 does say that if the unbelieving spouse decides to leave, the believing spouse is no longer bound; let him (or her) go and live in peace. This doesn't mean you try to drive him or her out! Your faith and your presence in your home may bring your unbelieving spouse to salvation; if he or she chooses to leave, you are free knowing that you have done what God told you to do. God has a plan for everything; don't try to tell me the Bible isn't relevant to today!

Back toward the beginning of this book, I began to outline ten things you would need to learn to do in order to produce successful results in your situation. You've come through nine of them so far. So what about Step 10? I saved that one for the last because it's the hardest and the longest step of them all. In the meantime let's just take a peek at what we've got so far.

In the beginning you made the shocking discovery that your spouse was addicted to or involved in pornography. Upon your discovery you probably tried to fix it yourself until you found yourself at the foot of the cross. Either way, that's where your journey to wholeness began. Even though God never told you to, you packed your suitcase with all of your resentment, fear, despair, an unforgiving heart, hate, uncertainty, pride, maybe some rebellion, and a few other heavy items that you thought you could bring on this journey.

This was the spot where your knees met the floor. Although it was the spot you might remember as being the worst part of the journey, in reality it was your first step toward the miracle your heart so desperately longs for. We all had to start at that point before we could make any progress at all.

Next, you began to understand that you had to remove some of the junk occupying your spiritual bags. So you opened up room in your heart for the Lord to begin filling your suitcase with the wonderful things you need to receive your miracle. You beefed yourself up with spiritual muscle and faith by tearing yourself away from focusing on your spouse's addiction and activities which gave you more time to focus on yourself and the Lord. Very good work on that step!

After that, you may have been tempted to stir the pot and try to get a reaction. We often feel a little too big for our britches at this point, and we will sometimes think we can say or do things to manipulate a positive reaction. Wrong! It was tough, but you managed to overcome that desire by giving it to God. Good job!

Knowing that the enemy is always trying to set you back and that you couldn't always be immersed in the problems that were swirling about your life, you found and retreated to your special God Spot. I'll bet that special spot gets lots of use these days! While retreating into the Lord's arms to recover from the attacks, you started studying your opposition. This gave you the wisdom you needed to recognize the lies Satan was telling you for what they were—lies!

The new armor of God you're wearing looks great on you and wow, you've become so talented with that Sword of the Spirit!

Fully armed and loaded with knowledge, you now have your Father's wonderful and unbreakable promises engraved on your heart; you even know the things you have to accomplish to receive them. The hope you have in that must make you feel like singing His praises every day! It is so much easier to deal with this situation when you're not focused on it all day and all night, isn't it?

How wonderful to begin to know that the people you love will be joining you on this journey. So you keep sharing His love while He keeps working on your situation to bring about perfect results! Can't beat that!

Little by little you're becoming a new person. The change in you is evident to anyone who knows you. I can only imagine how wonderful things are going to be when the miracle arrives and you start afresh! I'll bet it'll be just like a honeymoon all over!

You've got your armor on and you know how to chase the enemy away! Praise! Praise! Praise! for the One who has been guiding and teaching you. Be careful not to give the enemy any ammunition to use against you and your loved ones. Watch the company you keep and be on guard for those who do not know the Lord, especially if they (knowingly or unknowingly) allow themselves to be used to defeat God's children.

These steps are tried and proven. I've been using them for over six years and although they take time, when they are applied and followed to the best of your ability, the outcome is always successful. Always.

Why Isn't Some of This About "Them"?

You're probably wondering why we haven't talked a lot about the men who are addicted to pornography or why they are addicted. **This is because this process isn't about them.** It is about you and helping you survive the heartbreak that the addiction has left you with.

No matter what their reasons or the cause of their addiction, no matter what they say to try to convince you it isn't about you, I know and God knows that it has still left you holding a shattered heart. If that shattered heart is neglected, that leads to separation—not just separation from the one you love, but from the family unit itself.

The lessons you learn here and the lessons you will be blessed with from your Lord are meant to give you the power to be part of the solution and not the problem. It only takes a few good fights and an attorney to divorce the one you love. It takes a strong woman or man who is dedicated to the memory of what that love once was to fight for her or his family even when it looks like the battle may be lost. But you've allowed God into your heart to give you the strength to stand and fight, and it has been the power of your choice to do so that has set your course.

You chose to go down the less traveled path that takes the most effort, energy, and strength instead of the path that leads to nowhere. I am so proud of you! But better yet, Our Heavenly Father is proud of you for doing *His* business even when adversity was trying to convince you (and still might be trying to convince you) that you were going to lose.

You've really learned that embracing your victory forever requires a combination of everything you've learned thus far and applying that knowledge each and every day.

Embracing your victory means that once your spouse has returned to the marriage (mentally and in some cases physically), you will have to tune the enemy out and refuse to allow his "reminders" of what happened. You can't afford to let him interfere with what God is doing to make a new and better marriage for you and your spouse. When you are having a bad day, above all else resist the urge to remind your spouse that it was his actions that brought you to this point in the first place.

Always remember that forgiveness is the answer. Always remember that! John Scott once said that the religion of Jesus was the cross, not on the scales of judgment. Keep that in mind when you are tempted to judge your spouse for past mistakes. The Lord has forgiven him or her. So must you in order to make this work.

If You Can't Beat 'Em, DON'T Join 'Em!

Believe it or not, I have met numerous women who felt that after all kinds of nagging, threats, and silent treatments that the answer might be to try to get interested in pornography with their husbands. After all, the couple that plays together stays together, right? Wrong, wrong, and wrong! This is such a destructive idea that I can't even write strong enough words on this paper to tell you what a fall you're setting yourself up for if you go down that path.

Let me tell you the story about Cathy and Carmen. This couple had been married for a little over five years and after several situations that would have broken most couples, including a career change and relocation, they managed to stay married. Even though they had grown apart in some ways, they still loved each other deeply.

Cathy was a beautiful woman, but over the past few years the stress got to her along with the comfort of marriage, and she let herself go physically. Unlike when they were first married, Cathy didn't take the time to fix her hair before Carmen came home or put makeup on, and at night their intimate life had faded away to almost nothing. Exhausted from working and taking care of the children, Cathy would throw on her favorite holey night shirt, and fall into bed exhausted. Night after night, she would reach over to cuddle with Carmen and try to get things going, but he would reject her.

After about a year and a half of his rejecting her (and sometimes quite rudely), she was feeling pretty low about herself and accused Carmen of having an affair. She cried and yelled and accused and then became more upset when Carmen withdrew completely. Finally the situation reached a breaking point. Cathy was desperate to fix her marriage because she loved Carmen and, even though she didn't believe it, Carmen loved her very much. He just wasn't sexually attracted to her.

Carmen's solution wasn't to cheat; she sought instead to try to understand what this visual stimulation he was seeking was all about and how it might put him in the mood to be intimate. Carmen figured that the pornography couldn't hurt if Cathy was enjoying the benefits. Their sex life, Cathy told me, became better than it had ever been.

But disaster was bound to strike and it did. Answers built on evil never produce good endings.

Cathy slowly realized that all the fun they had been having over the previous months was not the solution she had once thought. She began to recognize that she was getting into bed with her husband when in reality he was getting into bed with the woman or women he had been looking at or talking to.

Who he thought about when he closed his eyes is what haunted Cathy the most. She finally called him at work and told him she was taking the children and leaving him. Carmen felt like a wall had fallen on him. He was losing the woman he loved and whom he had made a life with, the woman who mothered his children and whom he had plans to grow old with.

He raced home, praying he would be in time to catch her from leaving. He was, but it took hours of arguing and heated discussion late into the night about how they could rebuild all they had nearly destroyed.

Joining in the pornography is not an answer to any intimacy problem you are having. It's only going to ultimately make things worse. If you are thinking about this or are currently doing this, you may want to ask yourself a few questions. Are you okay with the fact that the sexual attention you might receive from your spouse is initiated or fueled by the thoughts of another woman? Nothing good or productive will come from sacrificing your self-respect and your self-esteem to allow this evil into your marriage willingly.

Did You Cause Their Desire to Trip into Pornutopia?

I ventured back into the land of Pornutopia for a different reason this time. It had been a while since I had gone into this area. The last time I visited a porn site, I owned it. This time my goal wasn't to make a profit, but to gather information. Once I convinced my subjects that I was serious about my mission, they surprisingly opened up and gave me a candid view of some of the reasons they were at that very moment seeking pornography.

I polled over one hundred men and three women about this topic. Everyone asked that I keep their identities private so all of the names have been changed at the request of the person being interviewed. The first person I spoke to was Daniel, a twenty-eight-year-old married man with a child on the way. He was in his first marriage. Daniel had pretty much the same story as most of the other men so I am using him as my poll example.

At the very moment that we were talking (about 11:00 P.M.), his wife was in bed sleeping with no idea that he frequented porn sites he had paid membership to access. He admitted to me that she would "freak out" if she found out he was actually talking with the porn models.

Daniel told me that his first experience with pornography was when a cousin shared a peek at a magazine filled with images of nude women in sexually explicit acts. He said that from that day forward, he couldn't get the images out of his mind and became obsessed with what he saw. Eventually he turned to internet porn to indulge his obsession.

This was not a scientific poll; it was just a way to hear it straight from the "horse's mouth" to get an idea of what some of these men are really thinking. After speaking to these guys, I believe without a doubt that there was a trigger in each of their lives that led to the addiction, all the way from being molested at an early age to being shown pornography while growing up.

So to answer your question (I don't know of a woman who hasn't asked this question) of what you did to contribute to the situation, I would say not much, if anything at all. So take off the guilt load you may have still not laid down completely, and let's look at some of the things that happen in a marriage that you can contribute positively to.

Step Number Ten: Sharing Your Support, Compassion, and Love with Him

Let's address the obvious first. If you know your spouse experienced some kind of emotional or physical abuse or trauma as a child that may be contributing to his addiction and he hasn't gotten professional help for it, sit down and talk to him about seeking help. A lot of men are hesitant to speak to anyone because they are embarrassed. If your spouse can be assured that he has your unconditional and nonjudgmental support in this matter, this can make a decision to seek help easier for him.

No matter how angry or hurt you are over his actions, you have a choice to put those feelings behind you and then sit down with him and gently guide and encourage him to seek help. You can let him know that you love him and you care about the demons he is fighting. Uniting with him in his fight can bring about unimaginable results.

Facing his dark side with someone who loves him makes it a lot less scary. Encourage him and build him up; don't berate and remind him of the destruction his habit has caused. Show him that you have changed and that you are standing by him. Help him to believe that your marriage and family are worth fighting for. Remember, not everything you hope for will come overnight, but standing by his side is a good step toward that answer. Always keep one hand in God's hand and you can't fail.

Take a moment to reflect on the reasons you and your spouse fell in love. Try to remember back to those first few months when you were together and you didn't think life could get any better than it was. I believe that a successful marriage always tries to retain its history and its beginning. After all, those were the most exciting times of your relationship. Talk about this with your spouse; remind him to think about how you fell in love, too.

My next mini-poll was performed in adult chat rooms—not necessarily pornographic, but geared toward adult visitors. After just observing for several evenings, I focused on five men who came back to the room regularly and spoke frequently about their wives. I explained what I was doing and asked them if I could poll them. They all readily agreed and were even excited to participate in my little experiment.

All five had been married for more than five years, but only three of these men had children. All five had careers in industries that required them to have at least a two-year college degree, and if they weren't lying, they were all making above $75,000 per year. All five men had looked at pornography in the past and still did occasionally. These five men all said their wives still interested them sexually, but not like they had before. Here are the reasons they gave as to why:

- She doesn't dress up anymore unless we're going out.
- She gained a lot of weight after having kids and never lost it.
- She isn't as sexy as she used to be and always wears these baggy shirts with sweat pants.
- I haven't seen her with makeup on in months.
- She doesn't do the things she used to do to initiate sex.
- She is always too tired.
- She started smoking, and I don't like the way she smells.
- She's been really mean the last few years. Change of life maybe?
- I don't think she tries to make that part of our marriage special anymore.
- How can you want to be "intimate" with someone who is constantly screaming at the kids and then at you?
- I don't want to make love to her. I want to hide from her most days.
- She always has a headache or she just isn't in the mood as much as she used to be in the beginning.

I asked the guys that if their wives were more like they were when they first met, would they be more interested in them physically. The answer was an overwhelming yes! The guys went on to share stories about their wives that they remembered from the beginning days.

Try to forget for a moment that your spouse may have let himself go, too. He may have bad breath and a beer belly, but he's still the man you fell in love with. Bad breath and beer bellies can change when God begins to restore him!

You can't change him, but you can change yourself. You cannot control your spouse's addiction to sex or his viewing pornography, **but you certainly don't want to add to the reasons that he turns to it instead of to you.** Take a moment to reflect on how you were with your spouse in the beginning and how you are now (minus the pornography issue). Are you the same woman with whom he fell in love?

All couples go through changes as time passes, but it takes an everyday effort to keep things fresh and exciting. Do your part to try to make yourself more fresh and exciting, and keep your expectations low at first. This will help you from being disappointed and wanting to give up. Do it for yourself; you'll find that it makes you feel better. As he does begin to notice, you will see some good reactions. Whatever you do, don't give up. Hang on to the Lord, and He won't let go of you. I promise!

When things get tough or you're having a bad day, visit the pornproofingyourhome.com Website for support and encouragement. I'll be there to help you through every step of the way. I've also included many resources for you in the last chapter and should you need it, help is always just a mouse click away at www.pornproofingyourhome.com — we're here 24/7 to help you get through. In concluding this book, I have asked Pastor Tom to finalize his thoughts:

Note from Pastor Tom: I have met a lot of people with a lot of problems, talked to a lot of families with a lot of issues, and counseled with a lot of couples who are perplexed by a lot of questions. Jack and Judy (not their real names) could never come to grips with the problems that were brought into their home by "unreal people" in pornographic photographs and movies, make-believe competitors with perfect bodies and fictitious personalities.

These unnamed and unreal "other men and women" never have to defend themselves and cannot be confronted in real life, in real time. They never have a bad-hair day, bad-skin day, or a bad day of any type. They seem to be perfect. They are the answer to every person's dream, but they are completely fake. They are fictitious impostors of the most heinous kind. They are perpetrating a fraud on poor, unsuspecting souls while real marriages are hanging in the balance.

It's terrible to lose a loving relationship to a real enemy, but to lose one to an enemy on a computer screen is the height of absurdity. Who are these fictitious people on paper and film who look so lovely and happy? It is all smoke and mirrors, but the problem is that the average Joe doesn't think about that. He dreams of "that girl" or she thinks of "that guy" and how "maybe someday it will happen to me." In the meantime, life goes on. Joe and his wife miss out more and more with every passing day while Joe keeps focusing on smoke and mirrors.

But you should now have the understanding to deal with this immense problem, dear reader. There is nothing that you—working with the Lord—cannot do. You plus God equal a majority! Turn to Him and thank Him for bringing you this far. You now have information on how to set up protection in your home. You now have doable steps to take so that you can surrender your situation to God and cooperate with what He will do to bring your miracle.

Get in a good Bible-preaching/teaching church where you can grow as a believer and even help others. Visit our Website and receive any more help that you need pornproofingyourhome.com. Thank you for allowing us into your home—and hopefully into your mind with the truth. God bless you.

Appendix

Where to Go For Help

No one can accomplish this journey without the help that is readily available to anyone and everyone who seeks it. I've used these links on various occasions for research and/or coaching purposes. I do not profit financially from any of the recommendations made. The resources and remedies you'll find in this section are also available on our Website pornproofingyourhome.com. Our website is updated regularly.

This mini-directory is alphabetized to make it easier to locate the resource you may be in need of.

Links marked with ☺ can be utilized for kids too.

Addiction: Sex/Pornography
12-Step Fellowships
- Recovering Couples Anonymous (RCA)
  http://www.recovering-couples.org/
- S-ANON Family Groups ☺
  http://www.sanon.org
  National 12-Step program for spouses of sexual addicts and partners of sexual offenders. Primarily married women in attendance. Companion program to SA. (615) 833-3152

- Sexaholics Anonymous (SA)
  http://www.sa.org/
- Sex Addicts Anonymous (SAA) ☺
  http://www.saa-recovery.org/
- Sexual Compulsives Anonymous (SCA)
  http://www.sca-recovery.org/
- Sex and Love Addicts Anonymous (SLAA)
  http://www.slaafws.org/

Addiction Resource: Sex/Cyber/Pornography

- SexHelp.com with Dr. Patrick Carnes
  www.sexhelp.com
- Dr. Doug Weiss at Heart to Heart
  www.sexaddict.com
- Online Sexual Addiction ☺
  www.onlinesexaddict.com/
- PureIntimacy ☺ (*author's favorite*)
  www.pureintimacy.org
- Focus On the Family ☺
  www.family.org
- The Sexual Recovery Institute

Anti-Spyware & Adware Resources

- Spyware Guide ☺
  www.spywareguide.com/
  Spyware Guide offers links to anti-Spyware software
  but also provides lists of companies distributing
  Spyware, and lists of software and applications
  known to contain Spyware.
- Security at Home: Fight Spyware ☺
  http://www.microsoft.com/athome/security/Spyware/
  default.mspx
  The Microsoft Security center provides detailed
  information on Spyware and tips and information on
  how to find and remove Spyware from your system.

- Anti-Spyware Top Ten Reviews ☺
  http://anti-Spyware-review.toptenreviews.com/
  Overviews and ratings of some of the most popular
  anti-Spyware software.
- Spybot S&D ☺
  http://www.safer-networking.org/en/index.html
  Spybot Search & Destroy can detect and remove
  Spyware of different kinds from your computer.
  Spyware is a relatively new kind of threat that
  common anti-virus applications do not yet cover.
- Ad-Aware ☺
  http://www.safer-networking.org/en/index.html
  Ad-Aware is designed to provide advanced protection
  from known Data-mining, aggressive advertising,
  Parasites, Scumware, selected traditional Trojans,
  Dialers, Malware, Browser hijackers, and tracking
  components.

Computer Software

- CyberSitter ☺
  www.cybersitter.com (instant download)
- BSafeOnline
  www.bsafehome.com
- NetNanny
  www.netnanny.com
- Cyber Patrol
  www.cyberpatrol.com

Kids: Keeping Them Safe Online

- Police safety Notebook
  www.ou.edu/oupd/kidtool.htm
- Government Cyber Security Tips
  www.us-cert.gov/cas/tips/ST05-002.html
- MSNBC Keeping Kids Safe Online
  www.msnbc.msn.com/id/3078811/
- Education World

www.education-world.com/a_tech/tech119.shtml
- NetSmartzKids
www.netsmartzkidz.org
- ThinkUKnow
www.thinkuknow.co.uk

What to Look for in Internet Filter Software

Even though the perfect Internet filter does not exist in today's marketplace, there are a number of great solutions depending on your family's needs. Below are the criteria TopTenREVIEWS used to evaluate Internet filter software:

- Ease of use. The most important attribute an Internet filter program can offer is an easy-to-use design, making it possible for people with all levels of computer experience to easily install and use the filter to its fullest capacity.

- Effective at filtering. Top Internet filter software offers a good balance between filtering objectionable material and not filtering too much content. Another important aspect is the ability to customize the filter's sensitivity for each family member.

- Filtering algorithm. The best filter programs use a combination of filtering techniques, including URL filtering, keyword filtering, and dynamic filtering.

- Activity reporting. The most useful Internet filter software offer reports on what each family member has been doing on the computer, which includes websites visited, chat room activities and so on.

- Client-Server based. Good filtering programs offer a flexible platform which allows users to decide whether their optimal filtering solution is client (home computer) based, server (Proxy or ISP) based or a combination of both.

- Foreign language filtering. Effective Internet filter programs offer the capacity to filter keywords in multiple languages. One of the tricks that many teenagers have discovered to bypass Internet filters is to type in the foreign language equivalent of certain keywords.

• Port filtering and blocking. Filtering programs should block or filter all major Internet protocols, including Web access, chat rooms, email, peer-to-peer networks, bulletin boards and popup windows.

With Internet filter software and proper supervision, parents can keep their families safe and sound from the ever-present problem of online pornography.

©2006 TopTenREVIEWS, Inc.

Kids: Safety & Reporting Cyber Crimes
• Safekids   www.safekids.com
• Protect Kids   www.protectkids.com
• ObscenityCrimes.org   www.ObscenityCrimes.org
• Cyber Tip Line   www.cybertipline.com
• Cyber 911   www.isafe.org
• National Offenders List
  www.registeredoffenderslist.org

Search Engines For Kids
• Bess The Internet Retriever   www.bess.bet
• Yahooligans!   www.yahooligans.com
• Ask Jeeves For Kids   www.ajkids.com
• AOL@School   www.aolatschool.com/students
• Cyber Sleuth Kids   www.cybersleuth-kids.com
• Kids Click   sunsite.berkeley.edu/KidsClick!
• Family Friendly   familyfriendlysearch.com

Video Game Reviews
• Game Rankings   www.gamerankings.com
• Video Game Review   www.videogamereview.com
• Video Game Critic   www.videogamecritic.net
• Our website   www.pornproofingyourhome.com

Wicked Web Words & What They Mean

I've put together a list of some of the most common words you'll run into when dealing with safeguarding your family from the evils of pornography. The list I have provided consists of the terms that you need to be wary of. These are the programs or situations that should warrant further attention on your part. You can check the pornproofingyourhome.com website for a regularly updated list as well as interactive help on some terms or software programs you might encounter along the way.

Most of the following definitions were obtained from the free online encyclopedia *Wikipedia* (found at wikipedia. com). This source is the most accurate for finding online terms and slang that may not be in a conventional dictionary or encyclopedia.

Adware—or **advertising-supported software** is any software package which automatically plays, displays, or downloads advertising material to a computer after the software is installed on it or while the application is being used.

Adware. (2007, April 9). In *Wikipedia*, The Free Encyclopedia. Retrieved 9:00AM, April 9, 2007, from http://en.wikipedia.org/w/index. php?title=Adware&oldid=120050341

Adult Oriented—is any web page that has content intended for adults (usually 18 or 21 years of age depending on the state you live in). These sites contain nudity, sexual situations, erotica and other content that is inappropriate for children, teens or tweens.

Blocking—is an action taken by software or simple programming to restrict access to certain websites or content found on the Internet.

Blog—is a web log, personal online diary or online journal that is presented in reverse chronological order that can be kept private or open to anyone surfing the Internet.

Database (Member)—is a structured collection of records that is stored in a computer so that a program or person can consult it to answer queries about members or other things.

E-mail—Electronic mail sent via the Internet.

Erotica—(from the Greek language *Eros*, "love") refers to works of art, including literature, photography, film, sculpture and painting, that deal substantively with erotically stimulating or arousing descriptions. Erotica is a modern word used to describe the portrayal of the human anatomy and sexuality with high-art aspirations, differentiating such work from commercial *pornography*.

Erotica. (2007, April 1). In Wikipedia, The Free Encyclopedia. Retrieved 13:07, April 9, 2007, from http://en.wikipedia.org/w/index.php?title=Erotica&oldid=119424205

Freeware—is copyrighted computer software which is made available for use free of charge, for an unlimited time, as opposed to shareware where the user is required to pay (e.g., after some trial period or for additional fuctionality). Authors of freeware often want to "give something to the community," but they also want credit for their software and to retain control of its future development. Sometimes when programmers decide to stop developing a freeware product, they will give the source code to another programmer or release the product's source code to the public as free software.

Freeware. (2007, April 8). In Wikipedia, The Free Encyclopedia. Retrieved 13:19, April 9, 2007, from http://en.wikipedia.org/w/index.php?title=Freeware&oldid=121125336

Internet or "Net"—The Internet is the worldwide, publicly accessible network of interconnected computer networks that transmit data by packet switching using the standard Internet Protocol (IP). It is a "network of networks" that consists of millions of smaller domestic, academic, business, and government networks, which together carry various information and services, such as electronic mail, online chat, file transfer, and the interlinked Web pages and other documents of the World Wide Web.

Internet. (2007, April 7). In Wikipedia, The Free Encyclopedia. Retrieved 13:26, April 9, 2007, from http://en.wikipedia.org/w/index. php?title=Internet&oldid=121002361

Instant Messaging—is a form of real-time communication between two or more people based on typed text. The text is conveyed via computers connected over a network such as the Internet.

ISP—An ISP (Internet Service Provider) is a company that collects a monthly or yearly fee in exchange for providing the subscriber with Internet access. An ISP might provide dial-up service, cable, DSL, or other types of Internet access. Some ISPs are local while others are national. A national ISP will provide access throughout most of the nation, while a local ISP will only serve subscribers in a limited geographical region.

From www.wisegeek.com

Malware—is software designed to infiltrate or damage a computer system without the owner's informed consent. It is a portmanteau of the words "malicious" and "software." The expression is a general term used by computer professionals to mean a variety of forms of hostile, intrusive, or annoying software or program code. In layman terms it means "virus."

Malware. (2007, April 8). In Wikipedia, The Free Encyclopedia. Retrieved 13:14, April 9, 2007, from http://en.wikipedia.org/w/index. php?title=Malware&oldid=121236007

Profile—personal information about a user or member of any given web community like MySpace, YouTube, etc.

Pedophile—is the paraphilia of being sexually attracted primarily or exclusively to prepubescent or peripubescent children. A person with this attraction is called a pedophile or paedophile. In addition to the generally accepted medical definition, the term pedophile is also used colloquially to denote significantly older adults who are sexually attracted to adolescents below the local age of consent, as well as those who have sexually abused a child.

Pedophilia. (2007, April 9). In Wikipedia, The Free Encyclopedia. Retrieved 13:32, April 9, 2007, from http://en.wikipedia.org/w/index.php?title=Pedophilia&oldid=121306101

Phishing—is a criminal activity using social engineering techniques. Phishers attempt to fraudulently acquire sensitive information, such as usernames, passwords and credit card details by masquerading as a trustworthy entity in an electronic communication. PayPal and eBay are two of the most targeted companies, and online banks are also common targets. Phishing is typically carried out using email or an instant message, and often directs users to a website, although phone contact has been used as well.

Phishing. (2007, April 7). In Wikipedia, The Free Encyclopedia. Retrieved 14:10, April 9, 2007, from http://en.wikipedia.org/w/index.php?title=Phishing&oldid=121057609

Predator—is an Internet user who exploits vulnerable people for sexual or financial purposes.

Shareware—is a marketing method for computer software. Shareware software is typically obtained free of charge, either by downloading from the Internet or on magazine cover-disks. A user tries out the program, and thus shareware has also been known as "try before you buy." A shareware program is accompanied by a request for payment, and the software's distribution license often requires such a payment.

Shareware. (2007, March 26). In *Wikipedia, The Free Encyclopedia*. Retrieved 14:14, April 9, 2007, from http://en.wikipedia.org/w/index. php?title=Shareware&oldid=117936522

Spyware—is computer software that collects personal information about users without their informed consent. The term was coined in 1995 but wasn't widely used for another five years, and is often used interchangeably with adware and malware (software designed to infiltrate and damage a computer respectively).

Spyware. (2007, April 7). In *Wikipedia, The Free Encyclopedia*. Retrieved 14:15, April 9, 2007, from http://en.wikipedia.org/w/index. php?title=Spyware&oldid=120996504

Virus—is a computer program that can copy itself and infect a computer without permission or knowledge of the user. The original may modify the copies or the copies may modify themselves, as occurs in a metamorphic virus. A virus can only spread from one computer to another when its host is taken to the uninfected computer, for instance by a user sending it over a network or carrying it on a removable medium such as a floppy disk, CD, or USB drive.

Computer virus. (2007, April 6). In *Wikipedia, The Free Encyclopedia*. Retrieved 14:17, April 9, 2007, from http://en.wikipedia. org/w/index.php?title=Computer_virus&oldid=120618309

The previous list gives just a few of the terms and definitions you should take the time to learn about. Knowing what these things mean will better equip and educate you in taking the necessary steps to protect your home and family from the evils on the Internet.

Be sure to check out our website
for an extensive list of terms and definitions.

pornproofingyourhome.com